UNDERSTANDING STEVEN MILLHAUSER

UNDERSTANDING CONTEMPORARY AMERICAN LITERATURE

Matthew J. Bruccoli, Founding Editor

Linda Wagner-Martin, Series Editor

Volumes on

Edward Albee | Sherman Alexie | Nelson Algren | Paul Auster
Nicholson Baker | John Barth | Donald Barthelme | The Beats
Thomas Berger | The Black Mountain Poets | Robert Bly | T. C. Boyle
Raymond Carver | Fred Chappell | Chicano Literature
Contemporary American Drama | Contemporary American Horror Fiction
Contemporary American Literary Theory
Contemporary American Science Fiction, 1926–1970
Contemporary American Science Fiction, 1970–2000
Contemporary Chicana Literature | Robert Coover | Philip K. Dick
James Dickey | E. L. Doctorow | Rita Dove | John Gardner
George Garrett | Tim Gautreaux | John Hawkes | Joseph Heller
Lillian Hellman | Beth Henley | James Leo Herlihy | David Henry Hwang
John Irving | Randall Jarrell | Charles Johnson | Diane Johnson
Adrienne Kennedy | William Kennedy | Jack Kerouac | Jamaica Kincaid
Etheridge Knight | Tony Kushner | Ursula K. Le Guin | Denise Levertov
Bernard Malamud | David Mamet | Bobbie Ann Mason | Colum McCann
Cormac McCarthy | Jill McCorkle | Carson McCullers | W. S. Merwin
Steven Millhauser | Arthur Miller | Lorrie Moore | Toni Morrison's Fiction
Vladimir Nabokov | Gloria Naylor | Joyce Carol Oates | Tim O'Brien
Flannery O'Connor | Cynthia Ozick | Suzan-Lori Parks | Walker Percy
Katherine Anne Porter | Richard Powers | Reynolds Price | Annie Proulx
Thomas Pynchon | Theodore Roethke | Philip Roth | May Sarton
Hubert Selby, Jr. | Mary Lee Settle | Sam Shepard | Neil Simon
Isaac Bashevis Singer | Jane Smiley | Gary Snyder | William Stafford
Robert Stone | Anne Tyler | Gerald Vizenor | Kurt Vonnegut
David Foster Wallace | Robert Penn Warren | James Welch
Eudora Welty | Tennessee Williams | August Wilson | Charles Wright

UNDERSTANDING STEVEN MILLHAUSER

Earl G. Ingersoll

The University of South Carolina Press

Published by the University of South Carolina Press
Columbia, South Carolina 29208

www.sc.edu/uscpress

Manufactured in the United States of America

23 22 21 20 19 18 17 16 15 14 10 9 8 7 6 5 4 3 2 1

Library of Congress Cataloging-in-Publication Data
Ingersoll, Earl G., 1938–
Understanding Steven Millhauser / Earl G. Ingersoll.
pages cm — (Understanding contemporary American literature)
Includes bibliographical references and index.
ISBN 978-1-61117-308-6 (hardbound : alk. paper) —
ISBN 978-1-61117-309-3 (ebook) 1. Millhauser,
Steven—Criticism and interpretation. I. Title.
PS3563.I422Z68 2014
813'.54—dc23

2013024194

This book was printed on a recycled paper with 30 percent
postconsumer waste content.

CONTENTS

SERIES EDITOR'S PREFACE

The Understanding Contemporary American Literature series was founded by the estimable Matthew J. Bruccoli (1931–2008), who envisioned these volumes as guides or companions for students as well as good nonacademic readers, a legacy which will continue as new volumes are developed to fill in gaps among the nearly one hundred series volumes published to date and to embrace a host of new writers only now making their marks on our literature.

As Professor Bruccoli explained in his preface to the volumes he edited, because much influential contemporary literature makes special demands, "the word understanding in the titles was chosen deliberately. Many willing readers lack an adequate understanding of how contemporary literature works; that is, of what the author is attempting to express and the means by which it is conveyed." Aimed at fostering this understanding of good literature and good writers, the criticism and analysis in the series provide instruction in how to read certain contemporary writers—explicating their material, language, structures, themes, and perspectives— and facilitate a more profitable experience of the works under discussion.

In the twenty-first century Professor Bruccoli's prescience gives us an avenue to publish expert critiques of significant contemporary American writing. The series continues to map the literary landscape, and provide both instruction and enjoyment. Future volumes will seek to introduce new voices alongside canonized favorites, to chronicle the changing literature of our times, and to remain, as Professor Bruccoli conceived, contemporary in the best sense of the word.

Linda Wagner-Martin, Series Editor

CHAPTER 1

Understanding Steven Millhauser

If ever there was a contemporary author who needed a book in the Understanding Contemporary American Literature series, Steven Millhauser is that writer. With the publication of his first novel, *Edwin Mullhouse: The Life and Death of an American Writer, 1943–1954, by Jeffrey Cartwright* (1972), Millhauser began a career that has stretched over four decades and includes a dozen novels, books of novellas, and collections of short stories. His reputation among writers and editors is very high, but he remains less known by readers in general than his fiction should have made him.

This disconnect between the high quality of his fiction and the absence of a reputation commensurate with his accomplishments has been noted by Danielle Alexander. In her hefty essay appearing in the *Review of Contemporary Fiction,* devoted to his writing, Alexander indicates that, as of 2006, in addition to "a healthy amount of book reviews" of his work, "there are five author interviews, approximately a dozen academic articles, a few book chapters, and two doctoral dissertations published in English that deal wholly or partly with Millhauser's fiction." Alexander argues that the author himself is partly responsible for this "lack of notice" because he "refuses to publicize himself, a consequence of his strong belief that an author's work should speak for itself."[1]

Alexander implies that Millhauser is an heir of the "New Criticism," generated by academics in the first half of the past century to explain the work of Modernist writers, especially poets. The "New Critics" encouraged readers to view literature as works of art to be interpreted *not* in terms of the author's life, the work's historical context, psychoanalytic theory, and so forth, but only in terms of the works themselves. Accordingly Millhauser has been less willing than many to talk about his own fiction, asserting that, if the work does not open itself to readers, the writer has failed and little can be said to make its meaning clearer.

Consequently Millhauser has been that rare contemporary writer who has made relatively little effort to "promote" his work. He has not sought out opportunities to make himself better known through an extensive series of readings, interviews, or book tours. Occasionally, as in his novella "August Eschenburg," he expresses the artist's need to resist the seduction of "celebrity." Once established, celebrity can tempt writers to become less scrupulous self-critics because they know that after they become a "name brand" their publishers can market *anything* they write. As the *New York Times* editors generalized of him: "A playfully reticent man . . . Millhauser is rarely heard from outside his fictions, seeming to prefer to reflect himself in tales as eerily distanced as they are lushly beautiful."[2]

Because he encourages readers to focus on his stories and novels themselves, providing a biographical sketch of Steven Millhauser has its challenges. When the *New York Times* was preparing a review of *Dangerous Laughter: Thirteen Stories* (2008), an editor asked by e-mail for a brief biography. Millhauser's response brought brevity to the maximum: "1943–."[3] In his novel *Edwin Mullhouse,* Millhauser reveals distinctly radical views of biography. He is probably aware of the jokes told about frustrated biographers who want to scoop others by publishing the first biography of their subjects but are apprehensive that their subjects might live too long, or at least long enough to change the course of their lives and render their biographies radically "incomplete." The optimal eventuality would be the fortuitous death of the author, just before the manuscript was ready for final revisions. Millhauser has even called biographers the "murderers" of their subjects.[4] Because biography is a text, it is a "fiction," despite its grounding in "facts." Biography ends up freezing the complexity and fluidity of its subject's life, reversing the myth of Galatea, the woman whose statue was brought to life by the love of its sculptor, Pygmalion. Biography "petrifies," turning living subjects into stone monuments.

For those readers who want and probably *need* to know something of Millhauser's life, we can provide somewhat more than "1943–." Steven Lewis Millhauser was born August 3, 1943, in Brooklyn, New York. His father, Milton Millhauser, taught at City College in Manhattan. When Steven was four, the family (including his younger sister) moved to Stratford, Connecticut, where the family settled after his father became a professor of English at the University of Bridgeport. Millhauser's mother, Charlotte (née Polonsky), was an elementary-school teacher. When Steven was fourteen, his family moved to Fairfield, Connecticut, where he attended Roger Ludlowe High School.

Millhauser completed a B.A. at Columbia College in 1965 and pursued a doctorate in English at Brown University during two stays in 1968–71 and 1976–77. He did not complete his dissertation, certainly no indication of his lack of scholastic talent or effort since his G.P.A. at Brown was 4.0 on a 4.0 scale. His interests were moving toward his own writing, for he wrote parts of *Edwin Mullhouse* (1972) at Brown and later wrote all of *Portrait of a Romantic* (1977) while living with his parents in 1971–76. In 1984 Millhauser married Cathy Allis; they have a daughter, Anna, and a son, Jonathan.

Career

Millhauser's teaching career began as a teaching assistant in 1976–77 at Brown where he developed and taught a course called "'Portraits of the Artist'—study in depth of works by Hawthorne, James, Mann, Joyce, and Nabokov." The author may have indicated these writers with some trepidation that the list would make his fiction the happy hunting-ground of academics bent on "explicating" it through his "influences." In 1986–88 he was a visiting associate professor of English at Williams College, before he became associate professor of English at Skidmore College, where since 1992 he has been professor of English.

Millhauser's career as a writer got off to a stellar beginning with his first novel, *Edwin Mullhouse* (1972). When it appeared, the writer Jim Shepard reports that within a week three writers called to urge him to read the novel.[5] Written as the biography of a child prodigy, who writes an alleged masterpiece before his death from a shot-gun wound at exactly eleven years, plus a few seconds, *Edwin Mullhouse* represents small-town American boyhood, as seen through the eyes of his eleven-and-a-half-year-old friend Jeffrey Cartwright, who is constructing a monument to a boy who might have written the "great American novel." Although its subject matter and mood are significantly darker, *Portrait of a Romantic* was also an (auto)biography, written by the twenty-nine-year-old Arthur Grumm, memorializing his friend William Mainwaring, who shot himself to death as an adolescent. Millhauser masterfully captures the tedium of high school and the boredom of endless summers before the electronic age. Although *Portrait of a Romantic* received mixed reviews, J. D. O'Hara spoke of the pleasant surprise that Millhauser had not disappointed his readers' expectations of a second novel as impressive as the first.[6]

Millhauser's third novel, *From the Realm of Morpheus* (1986), has a special place in his heart, in part because he worked on it for almost a decade and experienced difficulty getting it published. Chasing a foul ball, Carl Hausman, the narrator, finds his way down into the world of Morpheus, the god of dreams, who leads his young-adult guest on a tour of the underworld, the first major expression of Millhauser's fascination with subterranean worlds. *From the Realm of Morpheus* is a celebration of language, mainly Elizabethan English, but also Byron's. As *From the Realm of Morpheus* moved toward publication, Millhauser resisted Knopf's demand that its thousand-plus manuscript pages be reduced. Later he was forced to reduce the novel's length for its publication by Morrow.

Steven Millhauser's career is the exception that proves the rule of publishing fiction. Millhauser had published two novels and was working on a third before he began publishing short fiction. *From the Realm of Morpheus* came out in 1986, the same year his first collection of short fiction, *In the Penny Arcade,* appeared. Customarily fiction writers begin by publishing short stories in journals and magazines before a publisher is willing to invest in bringing out a collection of the author's short fiction. If a writer's first book manuscript is a collection of short stories, the negotiations for the contract may include the publisher's making a comment such as: What we would really like to see is the manuscript of a novel. For many publishers the acceptance of a writer's first book manuscript is an "investment," a gamble that the book will do well, followed by other books that might do even better. Books of short fiction, however, are even greater "investments," since they seldom sell as well as novels, even when the author is well established.

Millhauser indicates that, partway through the long effort to write and then publish *From the Realm of Morpheus,* he "allowed" himself to write the stories "A Protest Against the Sun" and "Cathay," which appeared in the August 31, 1981, issue of the *New Yorker* and the summer 1982 issue of *Grand Street,* respectively. In the years running up to the 1986 appearance of *From the Realm of Morpheus,* he published a second story in the *New Yorker* as well as stories in *Canto, Grand Street,* and *Antaeus.* With the exception of his first published story, "The New Automaton Theater," the other stories appeared in his first collection, *In the Penny Arcade.*[7]

Although he would publish a fourth novel, *Martin Dressler* (1996), which earned the 1997 Pulitzer Prize for Fiction, Millhauser is essentially a writer of novellas and short stories. In his 2008 *New York Times Book Review* essay, "The Ambition of the Short Story," Millhauser revels in the assets of shorter fiction, such as its "smallness [which] is the realm of elegance and grace." Taking his cue from William Blake's image of "All the world in a grain of sand," Millhauser argues for the "ambition of the short story" to be even shorter, to find the "single word," the "syllable" that would allow "the entire universe [to] blaze up out of it with a roar." Millhauser's interest in smallness is evident as early as his 1983 *Grand Street* essay, "The Fascination of the Miniature."

This essay is especially significant because it appeared about the time he was licensing himself to take breaks from working on his third, huge novel, *From the Realm of Morpheus,* in order to write and publish short stories in mass magazines such as the *New Yorker* and literary journals such as *Canto, Grand Street,* and *Antaeus.*

Like his two early novels, his first collection of short fiction was brought out by Knopf, a publishing house with a long-standing association with the best contemporary fiction. As Millhauser has indicated, he organized the collection in three sections so that the novella, "August Eschenburg," is balanced by the second section of three stories and in turn by the third section of three stories, an organization suggesting the author's interest in organizing principles suggestive of architecture. The second section includes "A Protest Against the Sun," "A Sledding Party," and "A Day in the Country," rendered a coherent unit by each having a younger female consciousness at its center. These three stories also form a unit as an expression of the literary realism to which he felt he was bidding farewell. This is not to say that the author was eliminating realist elements from his fiction; rather, as in "August Eschenburg" and at least two of the three stories in the third section, "Snowmen" and "In the Penny Arcade," he will ground his narrative in a scrupulously realist world, often with a plethora of details, then subtly move across an imaginary line into the world of fantasy. Increasingly, too, his narrative will become a variety of "fable," which book reviewers and academic critics have often seen as similar to the work of Franz Kafka, Thomas Mann, Jorge Luis Borges, Vladimir Nabokov, and Italo Calvino. His melding of realism and fantasy has also been called "Magic Realism."

In the Penny Arcade also provides an opportunity to observe not only the range of literary elements but the presence of the novella and short stories in his fiction. The novella's attraction for Millhauser is part of his method as a fiction writer. Contrary to the view occasionally encountered that the novella is simply an overgrown short story or a novel that the writer could not develop more fully, Millhauser is unambiguous about the three forms in which he writes. He claims that, when he begins writing fiction, he has a firm idea of whether the narrative will become a short story, a novella, or a novel. The novella, as he sees it, is a distinct form in the measure of its narrative development, even though he acknowledges that novellas are often identified by their word count. Because novellas are frequently several times longer than the average short story, journal and magazine editors are usually unwilling to publish them, requiring the author to bring out a novella in a collection of short stories or to bring out a collection of, say, three novellas, as Millhauser has done twice. Or if the author is particularly fortunate, a novella such as his

Enchanted Night can be published as a separate book. Given that a novella can be difficult to "place," Millhauser values the form because it carries a sense of liberation from practical concerns about where it might appear. He indicates that this circumstance allows for a greater sense of writing the novella for the sake of writing it.[8]

The author's second collection of shorter fiction, *The Barnum Museum* (1990), reveals clear advancements in his work. Among the most memorable selections is the novella "A Game of Clue," a brilliant fantasy, generated out of the board-game, played by four young adults on a summer evening. In *The Barnum Museum*, narrative moves beyond "In the Penny Arcade," where the story follows the pre-adolescent boy into a fantasy world and back out to join his waiting parents. In "Behind the Blue Curtain," whose structure recalls "Arcade," the boy's movement into fantasy is much more elaborate, in part because the viewpoint character is clearly adolescent. Reprising Millhauser's investment in childhood is the marvelous story "The Eighth Voyage of Sinbad" where a boy at a family picnic in southern Connecticut, perhaps near where the author grew up, is imagining Sinbad's eighth voyage, based on the principle that "there are as many voyages as there are readers" (138). And the collection's title story offers perhaps the fullest expression of the author's attraction to the subject matter and the form of narratives taking on a life of their own as they follow human efforts to construct ever more elaborate worlds, especially in large stories such as "The Dream of the Consortium" and "Paradise Park," and preeminently in the fourth novel, *Martin Dressler* (1996). The most memorable story is the powerful last selection, "Eisenheim the Illusionist," adapted for the screen by Neil Burger, as *The Illusionist* (2006), starring Ed Norton and Paul Giamatti. Born Eduard Abramowitz, in Pressburg (now Bratislava) Slovakia, Eisenheim became a master illusionist, who ends by making himself disappear.

The author's next book, *Little Kingdoms* (1993), offered him the opportunity to bring together three novellas. The first, "The Little Kingdom of J. Franklin Payne," unlike the second, "The Princess, the Dwarf, and the Dungeon," and the third, "Catalogue of the Exhibition," appears in this collection for the first time. Payne is a classic example of Millhauser's attraction to the overreacher figure, evident in his earliest published fiction, "The New Automaton Theater" (1981), "August Eschenburg" (1983), and "Eisenheim the Illusionist" (1984), as well as "Snowmen" (1984) with its passionate effort to create ever more intricate snow sculpture and "Cathay" (1982) in its creation of miniatures within miniatures. Payne is an overreacher in his refusal to use the "cel" technique of film animation, laboring instead at drawing each frame anew, a total of 4,000 separate frames to produce a four-minute cartoon. "Payne" offers a formative episode from the overreacher's boyhood to suggest that these makers are working out the fates revealed to them as children—August, Eisenheim, Martin, and others.

"The Princess, the Dwarf, and the Dungeon" offers an example of the author's attraction to the Middle Ages, evident in "The King in the Tree" and "In the Reign of Harad IV" (2006). The dwarf figure, a staple of medieval courts, is the only principal named—Scarbo—while the others remain generic—"Princess," "Prince," and "Margrave." As a husband consumed by jealousy and perceived betrayal, the Prince takes readers into the cellar of the soul and in part offers a counterpart to King Mark in "The King in the Tree" (2004), a husband whose dilemma is loving both his queen, Ysolt, and his nephew-rival, Tristan.

The third novella, "The Catalogue of the Exhibition: The Art of Edmund Moorash (1810–1846)," demonstrates the author's ingenuity in developing a unique method of narration. His narrator is the author of a catalog of entries for paintings in an exhibition devoted to the fictional American painter Edmund Moorash (1810–1846). Increasingly the unnamed cataloger departs from descriptions of the paintings (no visuals supplied) to focus on the artist's life, a blatant form of the biographical criticism Millhauser abhors.

Millhauser's next book is his fourth novel, *Martin Dressler: An American Dreamer* (1996), which earned him the Pulitzer Prize for Fiction in 1997. Although universally praised, the novel posed challenges for its reviewers as well as some academic critics, who have wanted to read it as a satire of the get-rich-quick-by-any-means entrepreneur. A careful reading of Martin in the context of Millhauser's other overreachers demonstrates the author's focus on the earlier notion of the American Dream as the quest for self-transformation, of leaving the Old Country for the New World in which we could dream ourselves into a larger spiritual state of being, thus recovering the Garden of Innocence. Martin is the American Dreamer as overreaching tragic figure, denying his father's resistance to "extravagance" to pursue ever more richly complex habitats for the human spirit. When his palaces generated by the energy of human imagination finally reach their inevitable limits and begin to collapse, Martin collaborates in his fall, for better to fail as a dreamer than to succeed as a complacent prisoner of the Old Country's little rooms.

The Knife Thrower and Other Stories (1998) has the feel of a larger collection than *The Barnum Museum* (1990), as that collection is clearly more substantial than *In the Penny Arcade* (1986)—even though the author's first collection has the powerful novella "August Eschenburg" at its beginning and the highly imaginative "Cathay" at the end. This density is hardly surprising in an author who by the turn of the century had published over two dozen stories and novellas. "Paradise Park" in *The Knife Thrower* seems "larger" because of both a length and a complexity of development qualifying it for novella status. Similarly the first published story, "The New Automaton Theater," is a big story in its intellectual density in contrast to "Claire de Lune" and "Balloon Flight, 1870."

"The Knife Thrower" sets the tone for this collection. The offbeat subject of an audience watching the knife-thrower's performance finds a perfect match in Millhauser's choice of first-person-plural narration to speak for a community attempting to puzzle out answers to a mysterious situation, as in "The Sisterhood of Night" and "The Slap" as well as in bigger stories, "The Dream of the Consortium" and "Paradise Park," where the question is: how immense and complex can a department store or amusement park become before it collapses?

Story after story demonstrates another facet of Millhauser's imagination, as it generates stories across a broad spectrum. At one end are stories such as "A Visit" and the ease with which the narrative slips from a familiar world into fantasy or "The Way Out" in which readers share the viewpoint character's amusement at an apparent entry to the theater of the absurd, which turns out deadly serious. At the other end are stories such as "Clair de Lune," with its actualizing of the "walking on air" trope in the airy, romantic mood of a fifteen-year-old discovering love; or "Balloon Flight, 1870," in which men are lofted above the earth to experience the world far above and the world to which the balloonists return; or "Beneath the Cellars of Our Town," which returns readers to the subterranean opened up in *From the Realm of Morpheus.*

Enchanted Night (1999) has the distinction of being Millhauser's only novella to be published as a book. This unconventional narrative suggests the late Renaissance masque as it moves away from realist fiction toward a performance with great emphasis on musical effects as well as visual elements on a summer night enchanted by moonlight. The narrative does have "characters," but they range from those who might have stepped out of "A Protest Against the Sun" or "In the Penny Arcade" to a store-window mannequin, dolls in the attic, Pierrot and his Columbine, a one-eyed cuddly bear, and night voices. Diana, goddess of the moon, chastity, and privacy is the "main character," however, for it is her moonshine enchanting those she has stirred from indoors.

Millhauser's second triad of novellas, *The King in the Tree* (2003), brings together three narratives of betrayal in love and the eternal triangle. "Revenge" starts the collection with a bang. The widow-narrator shows her house for sale to the "other woman" she encourages to join the straying husband in suicide. "An Adventure of Don Juan" moves the great lover, jaded by endless easy conquests in Venice to England with hopes of refreshing his amatory practices with more restrained ladies of the cooler North. Pursued by his host's wife, Mary, while he pursues her sister Georgiana, whom he discovers in bed with his host, Juan returns to Italy. In "The King in the Tree," King Mark is tragically caught between his "love for Tristan [which] runs so deep that it is like the love of a man for his own life" (148) and suspicions his nephew and his beloved Queen are lovers. Only their deaths can resolve the conflicts of the "eternal triangle."

Dangerous Laughter (2008) reveals another leap forward into his later approaches to fiction. "Cat 'n' Mouse," the prologue, draws readers into the author's rendition of the classic Tom and Jerry cartoons in which the clever mouse outwits the ceaselessly pursuing cat. Its dark ending prepares us for three quartets of stories with frequently bizarre subjects, and alien yet strangely familiar worlds.

The "Vanishing Acts" stories move toward greater complexity and subtlety, beginning with "The Disappearance of Elaine Coleman," a "mystery" in which the narrator discovers his own complicity, and ending with "History of a Disturbance," in which the speaker abandons communication because language is a barrier to direct sensory perception of the world. "The Room in the Attic" represents the author's continuing investment in the young adult's world; here the narrator, a high-school junior, is obsessed with the darkness he shares with a classmate's sister. The collection's title story offers another take on that young-adult world, in which the fad of laughter contests dissipates only after a young woman laughs herself to death.

The second section, "Impossible Architectures," follows a similar progression toward greater complexity. The speculative-fiction piece "The Dome" envisions an effort to enclose the planet in a biosphere. "Harad IV" provides another example of Millhauser's investment in the miniature, while "The Other Town" impresses the reader with yet another alternate world, a replica of our town, constructed not for habitation but occasional visits to the "other." It is "The Tower," however, which offers readers this section's most complexly developed expression of a most "impossible architecture" in Millhauser's completing the biblical Tower of Babel to reach the heavens, a tower so high that its top can be reached only as the effort of several generations of a family.

The last section's "Heretical Histories" provide their own share of surprises and familiar investments of the author, but with perhaps less of the discernible movement toward the complex. Accordingly, the closing story, "The Wizard of West Orange," focuses on the experimentation in Thomas Edison's New Jersey laboratory, more precisely experiments in haptography, to produce technological devices to replicate sensory perceptions. This fascinating story of an unnamed experimenter's work is told through his journal entries as he struggles to complete a haptographic body-suit to simulate sensation, a project aborted by Edison, the "Wizard," when it offends his moral values.

"A Precursor of the Cinema," a story approaching the length and complex development of a novella, works in a field familiar to Millhauser's readers—the pursuit of animation to represent motion, here the invention of "animated" painting. The story offers another example of this author's blurring of the traditional boundary between art and science/technology. "A Change in Fashion," the preceding story, may surprise Millhauser's readers in its subject of fashion design, but that field replicates the movement of hotel construction in *Martin Dressler* or Sarabee's amusement-park developments in an overreaching that inevitably collapses upon itself. It is the first of the "Heretical Histories," however, that may challenge the reader to the maximum.

As its title, "Here at the Historical Society," indicates, the first-person narrator is a staff member at a museum, which the reader discovers is dedicated to the "New Past." The museum's exhibits offer visitors "artifacts" of contemporary culture, with the potential to become future objects of our descendants' edification of our daily lives. The new concept of history is less interested in, say, Napoleon's sword than the average Parisian's shoes, just as historians today may be more interested in the daily lives of antebellum slaves than the thoughts of Lee at Appomattox. This noble effort to save archaeologists the effort of looking for our artifacts appears to have led to overreaching in the exhibits of Popsicle wrappers and cigarette packages, displayed here.

With the collection *We Others: New and Selected Stories* (2011), Millhauser's work reaches a milestone. The combination of "New and Selected Stories" reads in part as an acknowledgment of the three decades in which the author has been publishing stories across the spectrum of venues from the *New Yorker, Harper's,* and *Esquire,* to literary journals such as *Antaeus, Grand Street, Paris Review,* and *McSweeney's.* The "Selected Stories" segment of the collection reprints stories and novellas explored in earlier chapters; according to the author, if any changes were made they are so minuscule that even he could not pick them out.

Like "Cat 'n' Mouse" and "The Disappearance of Elaine Coleman" in *Dangerous Laughter,*[9] the first of the "New Stories," "The Slap," sets the tone of the collection.[10] It offers a classic example of Millhauser's later style in its rapid establishment of a familiar world—a "bedroom community" outside New York—into which an ordinary-looking, middle-aged man suddenly intrudes to eventually slap seven men and women without provocation or explanation. Accordingly the narrative is a mystery manqué to which the unwary reader may expect a traditional "ending," explaining who the slapper was, why he started and stopped slapping, and so forth. Instead, the reader needs to move away from "answers" to focus on the experience of a community—the narrator and other residents—confronting an enigma that is never resolved, as is so often the case in our "real world."

The other "New Stories" offer testimony to the wide range of the author's interests in and approaches to shorter fiction. At one end of the spectrum are short stories such as "The Invasion from Outer Space," a very different science-fiction story, and the moving story "Getting Closer" in which a boy refrains from beginning a greatly desired experience to savor the anticipation. There are stories such as "The White Glove" in which a teenage boy and girl have a bizarre relationship, recalling the couple in "The Room in the Attic," or "The Next Thing," an ominous dystopian world, extending from our mania for constant innovation. In its quasi-biblical context, "People of the Book" may recall "The Tower," another "fable," not of the Aesop variety.

The title story, or more precisely novella, "We Others," offers readers yet another classic Millhauser Tale, told by a first-person-singular/plural narrator, speaking for a "community." Once again, a story comfortably lodged in a familiar, "real" world gives way to fantasy and the supernatural, as the narrator reveals that "We Others" are ghosts. Soon the "familiar" world of ghost stories from Henry James's *Turn of the Screw* and B-grade movies is de-familiarized when Maureen, the woman of the house the ghost-narrator moves into, is not terrified but welcomes it/him. An overweight, unhappy, lonely elementary-school teacher, Maureen enjoys sharing her evenings with the ghost—she has soured on sex after her husband left her for another woman—until her niece visits, and Maureen finds her ghostly lover in bed with "another woman." Once again, the author's fertile imagination draws readers into experiencing a situation both alien and bizarre yet familiar to most.

Overview

Producing an overview of Steven Millhauser and his work is no small task. Given his distaste for discussions of his personal life as a serious invasion of his privacy and likely to result in the biographical criticism he detests, it is impossible to approach an overview from the conventional notion of influences. To advance the statement that he grew up in small-town America, specifically southern Connecticut, in the 1940s, '50s, and early '60s, the son of an English professor and an elementary-school teacher, would likely elicit from him a response such as: "So what?" Similarly, since his fiction has been likened to the writing of Thomas Mann, Jorge Luis Borges, Vladimir Nabokov, and Italo

Calvino, Millhauser, if asked by an interviewer about their influence on his early fiction, would likely respond: "Are you suggesting that a strong story such as 'August Eschenburg' is merely derivative Thomas Mann, or 'In the Penny Arcade' is warmed-over James Joyce? And you interviewers wonder why we writers grit our teeth when you ask questions!"

All this is not to provide grist for some mill whose intent is to demonstrate that Steven Millhauser is "difficult," at best, or angry and irascible at worst. What he has resisted throughout his four decades as a professional writer is the temptation to become a "public writer." As those who watch beginning writers in academe organize their game plans for becoming "successful writers" can well attest, some contemporary writers think of their "careers" in ways similar to the life-scheduling of aspiring movie stars or Wall Street stock traders.

Much of Millhauser's early fiction chooses as its subjects children and young adults for a variety of reasons, but certainly not to cultivate nostalgia and sentimentality. It is no coincidence that the author's first writer-figures include Edwin Mullhouse and Jeffrey Cartwright, pre-adolescents not looking forward to adulthood with great expectations but with dread. Much as they may seem precocious "authors," they believe, along with Millhauser, that all children are geniuses, but their "progress" toward adulthood necessitates the eradication of the very imaginativeness, creativity, or "genius" that qualifies anyone to become a writer.

Yet another object lesson is offered by Millhauser's story "In the Penny Arcade." Returning at twelve to the penny arcade after his last visit two years earlier, the boy-narrator experiences the disappointment he has scripted for himself: Among the automatons, the quick-draw gunslinger and the fortune-teller have devolved into so much mechanical junk, until the boy recognizes that they have not changed. He has. He has become "ordinary," like everyone else, perhaps to "fit in," and in the process gone "blind," lost the power to "see" as children see, with the clear vision that once powered the intensity of his creative imagination.

The Penny Arcade boy is not alone in the Millhauser galaxy. If the author's narratives of his artists' lives begin with their childhood, it is not simply that it seems the traditional point of departure. Artists such as August Eschenburg and J. Franklin Payne succeeded as adults because they were conservators of the child within—the child with the dynamo of imagination to make world-class automatons or exquisite animated cartoons. They became artists not for money, not for fame, but for the sheer, innocent delight of *making*. As Millhauser indicates, he got particularly attracted to the novella early on because he knew getting a novella published in magazines and journals could be difficult, if not impossible. Writing a novella could be like making a Tibetan sand-painting or carving sculpture out of butter—creating for the sake of creating and not for some extrinsic purpose.

In his early essay on the author, J. D. O'Hara spoke of Millhauser as a "mandarin." Like the attempts to position Millhauser within the context of earlier, and generally international writers such as Mann, Nabokov, Borges, and Calvino, O'Hara's "mandarin" label points to Millhauser's seriousness as a writer of "literature," as an "artist."[11] If such references have come to sound old-fashioned, even "elitist" in their suggestions that value in writing is less a matter of sales and celebrity and more about enduring artistic considerations, it may be a comment on fiction today. Millhauser swims against a tide of novels that have become less distinguishable from "airport novels" or novels begging to be reprinted with the tag "soon to be a major motion picture," with the promise of enough money and celebrity to guarantee the novelist will never receive another rejection slip. Novels in particular, because that is where the money is, have become as disposable as paper tissues—entertainments, serious or otherwise, to be read once and passed on to family and friends as a "good read." The traditional "gold standard" of "literature"—"fiction" included—based on the understanding that value inhered in a "work of art" being experienced again and again, even that the work existed as a *physical object* rather than a digital text the e-book reader can erase with a key stroke, is becoming as passé as a literary canon in which experts classed some works as more valuable than others. One suspects that some authors envy colleagues who are painters or sculptors because these "artists" know that "value" is financially determined by investors who expect a return on their investment and thus are more likely to buy a Van Gogh because the art world agrees on the excellence of his artistic accomplishments and are unlikely to "deflate" their judgment.

Millhauser may have done a service to those who are interested in his life as an author by avoiding the usual granting of an "Open Sesame" to his public through responding to questions concerning his personal life. By doing so, he directs his audience toward his fiction, where they discover projections of Millhauser in his "maker" figures, such as August Eschenburg, J. Franklin Payne, Kistenmacher, Harlan Crane, Graum, and others. The Millhauser who has seemed to some readers trapped in the past, given the settings of his many stories over a hundred years ago, is in many ways the historian of that period.

This Millhauser is evident in his idiosyncratic melding of art and technology, one of the most promising elements in his fiction. The frequent setting of his fiction 100–150 years ago is not evidence of the author's entrapment in the past, writing a variety of "historical fiction," but a fascination with the roots of modernism in the familiar conflict between traditional art and the burgeoning invention and technology of the later nineteenth century. The old chestnut that painting was irrevocably changed by the invention of the camera and advances in photography, moving "art" away from realism or representational art toward impressionism, post-impressionism, and so on, is a useful entry to Millhauser's investment in viewpoint characters such as August and Franklin as well as Graum and Crane.

If the conventional line of thinking describes traditional "high culture" confronting a growing chasm between art and the advance of technology, Millhauser is centered in figures, such as Harlan Crane, the artist-inventor, whose inventions will advance their art by expanding the possibilities of their technique. Crane invents a paint which animates the object in the picture. This "invention" may seem sheer fantasy, illusion, or "magic." But imagine the first viewers of film or listeners to the primitive phonograph, who probably considered Edison's inventions pure "magic." A "real" inventor named Harlan Crane may never have invented "animate paint," but Millhauser's creative imagination "invented" it, along with the technical finesse as a writer to encourage readers to temporarily suspend disbelief, as they were more capable of doing when they were children young enough to be this author's grandchildren.

Technology in the service of art is of course nothing new, for the development of oil painting in the Renaissance allowed painters to work on canvas for effects rendered impossible by the fresco method of tempera paints on fresh plaster. And it ought not to be lost on us that a great Renaissance painter such as Leonardo was also a gifted inventor and engineer. In his way Millhauser is resuscitating that tradition of artist/inventors for a historical period beginning in the nineteenth century and continuing into the twenty-first, a tradition of seeing art and technology not as enemies but companions.

Millhauser's attraction to a Franklin Payne inheres in the animator's role as an inventor of a technology for the representation of movement *and* as an artist who labors to create animation whose beauty will touch its viewer, rather than mechanically representing motion with no aesthetic dimension. The author's stake in this melding of art and technology is clearly its reflection of what he himself performs as a storyteller inventing new ways to tell stories and yoking those new methods, which create the pleasure of innovation for readers, with a mastery of language's capability to please the eye and ear. What Millhauser strives for is in part what he ascribes to Payne's artistic intent—to create the "poetry of the impossible."

CHAPTER 2

Edwin Mullhouse: The Life and Death of an American Writer 1943–1954, by Jeffrey Cartwright

From the full title of *Edwin Mullhouse: The Life and Death of an American Writer 1943–1954, by Jeffrey Cartwright,* readers expect a literary biography, complete with an apparent biographer, turning Millhauser into someone who "edited" the work for publication. Millhauser was well aware of the similarities between his surname and Edwin Mullhouse's. Because this was Millhauser's first novel, and first novels are frequently autobiographical, he is playing cat 'n' mouse with the reader who is ready to accept Edwin's childhood as Steven's recollection of *his* because both were born in 1943, the sons of college professors, and grew up in small towns in Connecticut.

But wait a minute, the careful reader may say; if I do the math, this "American writer" I have never heard of cannot have been more than eleven years old when he died! How much could he have lived, much less written, that could justify this moderate-sized book? That question of how an eleven-year-old boy can became a writer accomplished enough to justify a biography suddenly gets focused on the mystery of *how* he died—coincidentally or not—eleven years *to the minute* after he was born. Jeffrey as narrator is clearly anticipating the reader's challenge—Why am I reading the "biography" of a boy?—by identifying Edwin as a "boy wonder." Jeffrey is stressing the "*tragic* death" of America's "most gifted writer" to justify his project, yes; but he is also exposing his sense of comfort in having escaped the nightmare of biographers whose subjects are still living: Edwin is conveniently dead and thus cannot undermine the finality of the biography.

Because the first sentence of this novel makes the bizarre announcement that this biography's subject died at the tender age of eleven, the reader is immediately enlisted as a detective. We know the narrative will end with Edwin's death. Reading toward the end, we begin to gather clues concerning how Edwin died and how it happened that he died eleven years to the minute after his birth.

Some hints of answers are offered in the third chapter, when Jeffrey leaps forward to the summer of 1953, a year before Edwin's death, when the boys were ten, and Jeffrey was riding Edwin on his bicycle to White Beach. Jeffrey is "stunned" by how the amusement park has "changed" as a reflection of his lost childhood, forcing him "to see the long arcade of my childhood shrink to a dwarfish old age" (*Edwin Mullhouse* 9). Even more telling is Jeffrey's perception of Edwin as old, made miserable by his allergy, blanched as though he were looking out of an overexposed black-and-white photograph. Edwin's lapses of short-term memory of the park only two years earlier may be signs of early senility. After a long (over a page) sentence, Jeffrey recalls the two boys together in boats, rendered in the brilliant colors of a warm, living memory. The chapter ends with the image of Edwin as an aging child, "testily" asking, "'Can we go now? I have a splitting headache'" (13).

The impulse to write Edwin's biography will eventually become more clearly Jeffrey's misguided effort to rescue his friend from growing old by sealing him off hermetically in childhood. The biography is his mad strategy of preserving Edwin's and his own boyhood to celebrate its warmth and color from the inevitable bleaching into the black-and-white of aging and the diminution of childhood's larger, richer world. *How* Jeffrey will save his boyhood chum from the horror of that Paradise Lost of their boyhood together will be the story's climax of which these early chapters are the annunciation.

In this chapter from "The Early Years," Jeffrey is painting Edwin's and his childhood with Technicolor hues. "It was a brilliant day" (6) on which he rode Edwin on his bicycle to White Beach. Similarly, chapter 18 begins: "One sun-drenched morning shortly after Edwin's fifth birthday . . ." (76). Yet another chapter reveals Jeffrey's color-tinting as having moved into a surrealistic cartoon fantasy world: "It was a perfect summer morning. The sky had been soaked for hours in blue easter-egg dye and the grass shone like green cellophane" (25). Although it would be tempting to dismiss these graphic gestures as Jeffrey's self-conscious coloring of his childhood memories, they seem part of an impulsive need to accentuate the romantic aura of these lost boys' Edenic world before the Fall. Even more, they contribute to Jeffrey's obsessive effort to capture that lost world and to justify his desperate strategy of memorializing the Edwin whom he has paradoxically "saved" from the ravages of time.

These first three chapters certify Jeffrey's authority as biographer, even though Edwin would have quickly tossed the book aside as trivialized by its concern with "facts." Jeffrey denies he has the biographer's mania for facts, emphasizing how intimately he knew his subject. Despite such claims, Jeffrey is full of facts, such as his statement of his own age on Edwin's day of birth: "I was exactly 6 months 3 days old" (13). Jeffrey even seems ready to specify the number of hours and minutes separating the two. And surely Millhauser is having some fun at the expense of this "biographer" when he allows Jeffrey to hypocritically add that he makes no effort to focus on himself, merely offering "the pertinent details of a noteworthy occasion" (13).

Being a half-year older allows Jeffrey to pull rank in helping Edwin to "remember" how important his older friend was to his development. Jeffrey encourages Edwin to believe he recalls "meeting" Jeffrey as a baby and that Jeffrey was the first person into whose eyes Edwin actually gazed, before he "burst into a shriek of tears" (15). Perhaps even as an infant Edwin saw his future in Jeffrey's eyes. In any event the biography is now fully launched as the conventional travelogue of Edwin's infancy, whose authenticity is vouched for at the outset by Jeffrey's claim that after Edwin's homecoming from the hospital the two boys "were soon inseparable" (16).

Jeffrey is intent on demonstrating how their inseparability allowed him to know his subject more intimately than *any* earlier biographer could lay claim to. Jeffrey recalls being nine months old and listening to Edwin's infant babbling so perceptively that he can now "translate" it into adult discourse—for example, "*tatata* (singing)" (17). At one, Jeffrey claims the six-month-old Edwin's vocabulary included "words" such as "*chfff* (an earlier version of Jeffrey?)" (17), as well as "*keeeee*" and "*aaaaaa,*" sounds Jeffrey reproduces in stanzaic form, adding: "The astute reader does not need to be told that Edwin has just composed his first poem" (20). Millhauser may be offering here a pastiche of the baby Stephen Dedalus, singing an Irish ditty with a lisp and thinking, "That was his song" (Joyce *Portrait of the Artist as a Young Man,* 3). After a few pages culled from Edwin's "baby book," Jeffrey ties up the story of Edwin's first year by professing to be a prime influence "on the development of Edwin's style and soul" (*Edwin Mullhouse* 23).

Because Edwin will be *constructed* by his biographer as a great writer—what biographer would ever admit to choosing anyone less than a "great" as his subject?—language development in Edwin's childhood and an exhaustive compendium of the boy's reading are mandatory. Accordingly, over a half-page is devoted to all the books "Edwin is known to have owned between the impressionable ages of two and three" (40). For a time each was his favorite, but his "favorite of favorites" was *The Lonely Island* (44), a picture book with a single sentence or clause per page. Because this book had an "influence" on the great writer, the narrative reproduces the text from each of *The Lonely Island*'s forty-four pages.

Even in "The Early Years," Jeffrey is intent on amassing every possible expectation of the future writer. For example, Edwin's father, "in a spirit of glowing anticipation" of his son's future "masterpiece," attempts to read him his first comic book until Edwin quickly becomes so impatient that Mr. Mullhouse returns to "*The Littlest Injun,* Edwin's current favorite" (60). As a child over a half-century ago, Edwin experienced other phenomena influencing his later creative productions: "Comic books, cameras, photographs, Viewmaster reels—such were his simple games, but what omens for the omniscient biographer!" (62). That claim of omniscience is worth noting because Jeffrey implies he could offer up even more details of his subject but is resisting the conventional thousand-page biography.

Jeffrey also describes Edwin at five inventing a game after he noticed that he could slide the numbers designating grocery prices along the shelf edges, causing customers alarm when an item "cost" 73 cents, instead of 31. Edwin's biographer claims this long description of his subject's sequential movement of the numbers is justified by its foreshadowing of Edwin's "later delight in the art of artifice" (70). It also, of course, testifies to Jeffrey's vigilant surveillance and flawless memory of his subject's every activity, as each contributes to our anticipation of Edwin's becoming a "great writer," and Jeffrey an even greater biographer.

The reader's potential difficulty with Jeffrey's rendering of an episode such as Edwin's boyish prank of re-arranging shelf prices in the supermarket is worth pausing over because it reveals the complexity of Jeffrey's roles as a major character in a story he narrates. As in earlier episodes of his "listomania," Jeffrey's extended narration of Edwin's reconfiguring supermarket prices is intended either as a charming vignette of innocent boyish play or as an indication of the biographer's caressing these details as signs of Edward's anticipated "masterpiece." The problem readers find themselves confronting is the increasingly negative vibrations they are getting from Jeffrey as a pedantic biographer who cares less for his subject per se and more for himself by demonstrating his art in constructing the life of Edwin *less* as a master in the making and *more* as the biographer's creation. Once the author has delegated the narrator function to a character such as Jeffrey who is a "poststructuralist" for whom text is all, "Edwin" dissolves into the creature of his biographer's imagination. It is no coincidence that Jeffrey brazenly boasts to his subject that once Edwin is dead his only existence will be textual—Jeffrey's "biography." Once readers discover that Jeffrey has been responsible for

Edwin's death, and they recall Jeffrey's revealing boast about his biography, many of these representations of boyish charm are vitiated by the knowledge that Edwin never existed, except as Jeffrey's creation. As some actual biographies in which much is supposition, Millhauser offers readers an ersatz biography in which if the subject had not existed the biographer literally would have had to invent him.

Yet another omen of the dramatic climax of Edwin's life and Jeffrey's biography is suggested in a short chapter, beginning: "I wonder if I have sufficiently emphasized a major theme of this biography." Jeffrey continues: "I refer to Edwin's naturalness, his distinct lack of what is usually called genius" (74). The biographer has more than one ax to grind here. Jeffrey will not only suggest that "genius" is synonymous with "naturalness" but also that were it not for this biography and the Edwin he preserved/constructed in it his friend's genius would have been eradicated by the process of maturation. More importantly Jeffrey reveals an idiosyncratic definition of genius that will illuminate his later action in this novel and foreshadow the genius of other Millhauser "artists," of one kind or another.

Jeffrey points to Edwin as the prototype of millions of other children with immense creative imagination. Among hordes of bright children, Edwin was an exception in "the stubbornness of his fancy, his unwillingness to give anything up," and his "capacity to be obsessed" (75). The biographer generalizes that children are "geniuses . . . but sooner or later it is beaten out of us, the glory fades, and by the age of seven most of us are nothing but wretched little adults" (75). Jeffrey adds that he and Edwin talked about the inevitability of losing that "capacity to be obsessed" and "the advantages of suicide" (75), leading Jeffrey to remark on "the bitterness of [Edwin's] smile as I spoke with unusual magnificence of what I called, in a memorable phrase, the obscenity of maturity" (76). Clearly Jeffrey the narrator, who knows how this story will end, because the "plot" was finished before the narration began, is foreshadowing Edwin's ending with a vengeance. He is even exposing the distinct possibility that it is he, more than Edwin, who preserves "genius" through a "capacity to be obsessed," a capacity many would call insanity.

A key episode in the remainder of "The Early Years," or first six years of Edwin's life, fully a third of the book, introduces a character who will have tremendous "influence" on Edwin's becoming a "child prodigy." This new character appears after Edwin goes missing for a time in a chapter that ends with a cliffhanger assertion: the boy with his back turned, thought by both Jeffrey and Mrs. Mullhouse to be Edwin, was *not.*

The young look-alike is Edward Penn.[1] "Penn" is seven and lives in a "world of make-believe" so infinitely gratifying that he has little interest in anything outside his "heated cellar"[2] with its "treasure-house" of comic books. Penn is trying his hand at animation, offering Edwin and Jeffrey samples of "flip books," precursors of cinema. Edwin is fascinated with Penn's world and anxious to visit again, but the Penns live too far away, and Mrs. Mullhouse is not keen on visiting Penn's elderly parents, who speak of nothing but their illnesses. Penn himself is a reluctant host, saying little and evidencing a phobia of noises. Although the third visit is more successful, Jeffrey surmises Penn is more affable because he knows this will be their last, as indeed it is. Despite Mrs. Mullhouse's repeated calls to ask to visit, Mrs. Penn always demurs, saying her son is "indisposed." Years later, the boys walk past the now-abandoned Penn house, with its mysteries of not only the family's disappearance but whether they were ever actually there.

Penn's chapter begins with Jeffrey's characterizing the strange boy as a figure from *Alice's Adventures in Wonderland,* such as the March Hare or the Mad Hatter. It ends with Jeffrey's last image of Penn at the bottom of the cellar stairs in the darkness, having "faded almost completely away," like the Cheshire Cat of *Alice's Adventures in Wonderland.* All that is visible in the cellar's darkness is "the vertical row of white buttons on his shirtfront, glowing like miniature moons" (93), suggesting a phantom about to return to the spirit world. He has served his narrative function of infecting Edwin with the contagious obsession with comic books and animation that will eventually generate Edwin's "masterpiece." Edwin later affirms Penn's function by saying of the three influences in his life that "only Edward Penn had left a lasting mark," impelling the vain Jeffrey to ask, "And the other two?" assuming Edwin would name his future biographer as one of them. When Edwin answers, "Rose Dorn and Arnold Hasselstrom," and blushes with embarrassment at his obvious omission, "and you too, Jeffrey," Jeffrey tries to put the best face on Edwin's slight by joking, "Mathematics was never your strong point, Edwin." Edwin is left bewildered, impelling Jeffrey to remark that "Edwin was never one to understand other people's jokes" (81). Edwin's creating of this embarrassing episode may also be Jeffrey's means of establishing Edwin's independence from his biographer's construction of him, rather like the ventriloquist's time-worn strategy of having the dummy mock him with a critical remark.

"The Early Years" section closes by focusing on biography. "The fatal flaw of all biography, according to its enemies," Jeffrey begins, "is its helpless conformity to the laws of fiction" (100), everything contributing to "a foreknown climax" of the "hero's life." To Edwin, who once dismissed biography as "so simple. . . . All you do is put in everything" (100), Jeffrey poses the question: "isn't it true that the biographer performs a function nearly as great as, or precisely as great as, or actually greater by far than the function performed by the artist himself? For the artist creates the work of art, but the biographer, so to speak, creates the artist. Which is to say, without me, would you exist at all, Edwin?" (101–2).

This passage also foreshadows the biographer's Prometheus complex—his arrogant self-delusion of constructing the artist-subject. Even more ominous is the closing image of "the hot lamp where a trapped moth was stupidly beating its wings," a trope of Edwin as the biographer's subject who will struggle futilely against the incinerating future in which he will die as a sacrifice to his biographer's lethal embrace. In lecturing Edwin that his biography can have a "design" only if it has an end to complement its beginning and middle, Jeffrey presumes his subject understands what that inescapable ending entails. The very end of the passage is Jeffrey's focusing on "one of those curious tricks of the senses" by which the reflection of the dying moth in Edwin's glasses makes his biographer imagine he hears "faintly in that prophetic silence [of Edwin], the sound of wings beating madly in his eyes" (102).

Edwin's earlier remark that Rose Dorn and Arnold Hasselstrom were among the trio who "exercised an influence on his life" offers a segue into "The Middle Years," much of which is invested in Edwin's intense engagement with those two figures. In retrospect, readers may sense that Penn's function is not merely to explain Edwin's obsessive attraction to comic books but also to diminish the "influence" of Rose and Arnold, who come into Edwin's life in his middle years as classmates and are gone by the end of that segment. Also like Penn, Rose and Arnold are challenges to Jeffrey as Edwin's friend and biographer, since obviously he is jealous of Edwin's puppy love for Rose and his inexplicable affection, if not reverence, for the brutish Arnold.

This Rose Dorn, or "Thorn Rose," segment of "The Middle Years" becomes painful and yet all too familiar as a conventional rendition of "puppy love." Jeffrey's obvious jealousy heightens Edwin's unrequited "love," since presumably his biographer has never felt that way about a girl, or anyone else. Jeffrey's description of Rose is telling. She is a "bold little hussy," a term his mother or grandmother might have used but hardly a term in a twelve-year-old's vocabulary. He speculates that Rose never returned Edwin's affection but "actually disliked him from the start" yet "loved to be loved. . . . Edwin's fascination fascinated her" (141), the implication being that Edwin may not have ever loved Rose but only loved loving her.

The rendering of Edwin's juvenile "poems" to Rose, her humiliation of him, and her ultimate rejection of her suitor are probably colored by Jeffrey's jealousy and the suspicion that she is deliberately attempting to separate him from his friend. Her challenges to his efforts as biographer appear when he allows the mask of "objectivity" to slip: "I never liked Rose Dorn; but I do not wish to temper the strict truthfulness of this biography by painting her one stroke blacker than she was." Struggling to find something positive to say, he adds: "She did not always torment us. . . . I suppose she left us alone" (176). Perhaps Jeffrey is making an effort to restrain his hatred for Rose because he is about to describe her end. It is a mysterious ending, resulting from Rose's sadistic disruption of their teacher's leading the class in the Lord's Prayer, each disruption more flagrant until the day when the class hears a fire engine and sees smoke in the distance. Jeffrey offers a bizarre final conclusion regarding Rose: "She died two days after the death of her hair" (179), presumably turning her death into the ultimate act of spite by removing herself as an object of Edwin's affections—setting her own hair on fire.

The episodes involving Arnold Hasselstrom provide even greater challenges to the biographer. Rose Dorn at least was a girl, and Jeffrey can tolerate his friend's mooning over Rose because Edwin is performing the male role. Edwin's fascination with Arnold is more unsettling because "Hass" threatens to supplant Jeffrey in the circuit of Edwin's affections. When Jeffrey knocks on Edwin's bedroom, "followed by a longish pause, broken by faint movements," Edwin's "'Come in'" is spoken "without enthusiasm" (204). After Jeffrey meticulously details what he earlier saw, he asserts point-blank, "On the far side of the bed sat Arnold Hasselstrom" to whom Edwin says, "Oh, it's only Jeffrey" (204).

At the outset Jeffrey announces the relationship as "the ill-starred friendship between Arnold Hasselstrom, that disobedient boy, and obedient Edwin" (204). After marketing himself as Edwin's biographer, who knows his subject more intimately than anyone else, Jeffrey joins the reader in suspecting that something illicit, perhaps sexual,[3] was interrupted by his knocking. It appears, however, to be "only" the hunting knife that Edwin wanted to conceal from his family. Additionally the "only Jeffrey" is not a put-down, but probably an expression of relief that it was not Mrs. Mullhouse at the door.

Jeffrey has hardly introduced Arnold Hasselstrom before making it clear that he and Edwin's new friend are bound in mutual hatred. Tellingly the biographer does not refer to his rival as "Arnold," the way their teacher addresses him, or as "Hass," his preferred nickname, but as "Arnold Hasselstrom," distancing him as the interloper of whom he is clearly jealous. Indeed he seems to detest his enemy so vehemently that he fails to see that Rose and Arnold Hasselstrom are the same figure transgendered. Edwin is attracted to both from some discernible unease about the comfort of his privileged life in a *Father Knows Best* family in which "Dr. Mullhouse" is a college professor, Mrs. Mullhouse is a loving mother and model homemaker, and Karen is the lovable "kid sister." Although Jeffrey suggests he could dispute it, Edwin is top of his class, as well as popular and respected, even though not particularly athletic. Alternatively Rose may represent the more conventionally "feminine" end of the gender spectrum—love and sentiment—while "Hass" is the aggressive "masculine" end—brute strength and violence—to which Edwin may be secretly attracted as a space outside the cozy, "perfect-family" context he finds inhibiting. In any case Edwin's relationships with both Rose and "Hass" have elements of a self-punishing streak in Jeffrey's subject that will eventually attract him to suicide, like later Millhauser characters who are bored with the tedium and sameness of their comfortable lives.

Arnold Hasselstrom and Edwin may indeed bond in large part because beneath their superficial differences the two boys are soul mates. This identification becomes especially evident for Edwin in their "borrowing" and gifting, as he continues to force "loans" on Arnold of prized possessions such as valuable, rare comic books, even though he knows full well that Arnold may never return them. Edwin's self-punishing behavior is only magnified in the sociopathic Arnold's behavior that must ultimately end in his death in violent fights with older boys or skirmishes with the police. He claims that Arnold Hasselstrom's role in the biography is justified only by his importance to Edwin's imagination, and yet Jeffrey clearly relishes writing off the life of his rival for Edwin's affection and returning to sole possession of his friend as biographical "subject."

"The Middle Years" section ends with Jeffrey's commentary on the "over two hundred cartoons" he and Edwin saw together, once again stressing his intimacy with his subject's experience, especially as it contributed to Edwin's "masterpiece." And of course Jeffrey has to list the titles of almost all of the two hundred. He goes on to note Edwin's last piece of "juvenilia, a poem dedicated to Arnold Hasselstrom, which Jeffrey cites not only to emphasize his "objectivity" in including this forerunner of *Cartoons* but also to celebrate Arnold's death, for Edwin would never have dedicated the poem to a living "Hass."

"Part Three: The Late Years" begins with a sense of its "late"-ness, as Jeffrey self-consciously moves toward the end of his subject's life. It is September (1952) again with its sense of déjà vu for the biographer. Edwin is "in love" again, and Jeffrey is intent on helping "to guard him against enchantment with all means at my disposal" (227). After pages of describing his effort to find out which of four girls Edwin is mooning over now, Jeffrey is relieved—no more than the reader—to discover that his subject is passionately involved with not a girlfriend but the composition of his future masterpiece, *Cartoons.* What's more, Edwin's puppy love has been a hoax whose revelation makes him erupt "into screams of laughter" (235), and Jeffrey feels the need to justify his extended narration of his machinations with the four girls to argue that Edwin really was "in love," but it was another kind of love, essentially a "higher love."

In seeking seclusion to write, Edwin sets in motion his biographer's plan to corral his wayward friend into becoming his subject in that "bright, dark spring of 1953" (245). Jeffrey explains that it was the pain of his subject's absence which eventually made him suddenly recognize he was going to write Edwin's biography. Jeffrey allows the mask to slip as he reveals how the biography gives meaning to his life, and continues: "Mountainous meditations, you say, for so modest and molehillish a biographer. And why not? After all, there was nothing else to do" (246). Thus Jeffrey becomes the first of the Millhauser children to resort to increasingly bizarre strategies and activities to confront the fundamental fact of childhood—boredom.

In his last year Edwin's immersion in the writing of *Cartoons* pushes Jeffrey toward neurotic personification of its manuscript as a "jealous" lover, "resentful of Edwin's recent affection for his old friend" (250). It "began to punish him cruelly, teasing him and tormenting him and mocking him and making him suffer such black despair, such crimson agony, as Rose Dorn had never inspired" (250). Jeffrey's piling up of sadistic predicates here reveals less about Edwin's state than Jeffrey's jealousy and resentment. Edwin, whom Jeffrey seeks to possess, is betraying his affection so strongly that Jeffrey finds himself enjoying the wayward sufferer's pain. And of course Jeffrey enjoys moving forward the plot by which he will finally *possess* his subject in the cage of his biography.

Not, however, until Edwin finishes his masterpiece in his last March will Jeffrey finally disclose his planned biography. The two walk home from school on a windy afternoon, making it difficult for Edwin to make out Jeffrey's excited praise of his manuscript. Additionally Jeffrey discloses his "shyness" in moving toward an announcement of the biography, in part because lack of sleep has produced in him an "intense nervous agitation . . . like a wider waking" (269). It is not until they have reached the inner sanctum of his subject's room that he "blurt[s] out: 'Edwin, I'm going to write your biography'" (269). For the first time Jeffrey is *extremely* uncomfortable in his friend's bedroom, as marked by his observing that "modest Edwin stepped into his closet to change into his playclothes." The suggestion seems less a hint of incipient homosexuality than Jeffrey's sense that writing a friend's biography is tantamount to violating the privacy of another's innermost being. When he fears he spoke too softly or unclearly for Edwin to hear him and "in anguish and anger" repeats himself, his subject rebukes him for shouting, adding, "Anyway, how can you write my biography. I'm not dead." Ominously Jeffrey responds: "'You don't have to be dead,' I sneered, though as it turned out I was mistaken" (270).

Edwin's response to the biography soon becomes "passionate regard," similar perhaps to his sadistic pursuit of Rose Dorn or the passionate affair with the manuscript of *Cartoons,* which threatened always to elude his possession. But then this "passion" for his biography, like the Rose and *Cartoons* affairs, may have its roots in what Jeffrey bluntly asserts: "Edwin was bored" (270). In that boredom Edwin amuses himself with playing the subject of his biography, even entertaining thoughts of the conventional biographer's concern with the incompleteness of a living subject's biography: "Jeffrey, suppose a person knew the day he would die" (278), setting the wheels turning in his mad biographer's psyche on how he might encourage his subject's suicide.

Now comes the difficult part—Jeffrey's narration of the last hours of Edwin's life. The narrative becomes increasingly ominous as Edwin and Jeffrey "play" at scheduling Edwin's shooting himself at 1:06 P.M., exactly eleven years to the minute after he was born. Increasingly readers sense that Edwin may think he is playing a game of attempting suicide for the benefit of his biographer, whom he accuses of being "serious," but Jeffrey is "deadly" serious about this game they are playing because Jeffrey has "given away the ending." Jeffrey is "serious"; that is, he does not join Edwin in hamming up his role by pleading with Edwin to put the gun away. In fact, when Edwin returns from the bathroom where he went to change into his pajamas, he discovers his biographer in the closet, "Looking for—looking for—" (29). After Edwin quickly finds the gun, Jeffrey tells him he also needs the ammunition "clip," or, as he corrects himself after surmising he should not know too much about weapons, the "other thing" (294). If this is boys' play, why does the revolver need to be loaded? Jeffrey wrote earlier that his "self-doomed friend" is "deluded" by "grave errors" concerning biography. The biographer does not cram every detail in but is "highly selective" and has no more interest in the latter days of his subject than in the earlier. But Jeffrey details extensively everything he finds instead of the revolver in Edwin's closet, just as he details everything he packed in his overnight bag for his witnessing of his friend's suicide.

The suspense mounts as we feel trapped in Edwin's bedroom and drawn irresistibly to Jeffrey's participation in/observation of a suicide as he counts down to "zero" at 1:06 P.M. Now comes the really difficult point for readers, as Edwin raises the revolver to his temple and *says,* "'Bang, I'm dead,' . . . clutching the silent gun," before "his eyes opened and he said, 'Now what'" (301). It would appear the gun is not "silent" *after* it was fired but still silent because it was *not* fired. In the chapter's devastating final sentence Jeffrey describes how it took only "a split second" for his "gripping [Edwin's] gun-gripping hand" to finish the job, reassuring himself that the record of Edwin's birth at 1:06 P.M. "allowed leeway in the matter of seconds" (301). The height of Jeffrey's madness is the concern that his subject may have died a few seconds "late," and thus messed up the neatness of the biography.[4]

Several readers have found this ending surprisingly difficult. The first significant article, by Timothy Adams (1982), had no difficulty with the ending, asserting that "the biographer murders his own subject for artistic effect and a smooth ending" (213).[5] While reviewing *In the Penny Arcade* (1986), David Leavitt comments upon the reissue the same year of *Edwin Mullhouse,* whose ending he surprisingly misreads: "In an almost Mishima-like act of planned suicide, Edwin has shot himself on the eve of his eleventh birthday . . ." (117). Although he cites Adams but not Leavitt in his 1988 *Biography* article, the critic John Boyd argues for Edwin's "ambiguous death," and attempts to clarify that ambiguity by arguing that the reader is "uncertain whether the event constitutes reality, game, or dramatic performance" (44), as though it could not be all three. Boyd agrees with the early reviewers who saw Edwin's refusal to commit suicide eventuating in "his murder by Jeffrey" (44), but then obfuscates that actuality by also looking at the event as biography itself being a form of murder. What Boyd implies are mutually exclusive readings do not deny each other's legitimacy.

The confusion proliferates in later readings of *Edwin Mullhouse.* Although Douglas Fowler in his 1996 *Critique* article does not cite Adams, Leavitt, or Boyd, he nevertheless advances the continuing (mis)reading that "Edwin Mullhouse, now abandoned by his 'immortal masterpiece' after he has completed *Cartoons,* kills himself on his eleventh birthday . . ." (140). As late as 2002 Alejandro Herrero-Olaixola in his *Mosaic* article follows Boyd's confusion, writing: "The suicide, originally thought of as a mere simulation enacted for literary purposes, results in Mullhouse's mysterious death . . ." (77). Danielle Alexander (2006) and Catherine Kasper (2009) accurately read Edwin's death as murder by Jeffrey. To remove any lingering doubt, however, we might do well to give the author the last word.

Some years ago while corresponding with Steven Millhauser, I mentioned that my reading of Jeffrey's murder of Edwin seemed not to be shared by others who had written on the novel. The author wrote: "Just to set your mind at rest: yes, Jeffrey is the murderer. I'm pleased you saw that. Many people have misread the ending, which for me is crucial: a biographer, my cruel book suggests, is someone who murders his subject. The book is Jeffrey's oblique confession."[6]

CHAPTER 3

Portrait of a Romantic

The success of Millhauser's first novel, *Edwin Mullhouse,* contributed measurably to the favorable response to *Portrait of a Romantic* (1977).[1] The novel begins fittingly in an unnamed Connecticut town,[2] as did the first novel, and clearly this second novel is exploring another part of Millhauser country. The narrator, twenty-nine-year-old Arthur Grumm, is an older version of Jeffrey Cartwright, attempting to pass off a "fiction" as a memoir, rather than a biography. Thus, like Jeffrey, Grumm is a "character" in his own text, a hybrid of the novel and (auto)biography/memoir. Eventually Grumm reveals he is telling this story because he too has committed a crime for which he shares some of Jeffrey's ambivalent feeling of guilt and innocence.

Because Arthur Grumm is an adult, not the eleven-year-old Jeffrey, he begins by summarizing his early life. Obviously Grumm has no need to describe in detail the territory of his pre-adolescent life because he has the larger territory of his adolescence to cover, and it clearly is the adolescent Arthur who is the subject of the story. In contrast to Jeffrey's telling the story of how he "assisted" Edwin's "suicide" fairly soon after the event, Grumm is narrating his story well over a decade after he was responsible for William Mainwaring's actual suicide. Thus, as Danielle Alexander notes,[3] *Portrait of a Romantic* begins with two Arthur Grumms—the narrator/novelist/memoirist and the character in that text.

This sense of two Arthur Grumms is established by the first pages of *Portrait of a Romantic.*[4] The storyteller Grumm offers up verbal extravagance in his opening pastiche of Walt Whitman's style: "Mother of myself, myself I sing: lord of loners, duke of dreams, king of the clowns" (*Portrait of a Romantic* 1). Grumm is the "mother," or progenitor, of himself, both as the boy he is creating, based on the historical "Arthur Grumm," and as the adult storyteller Grumm who is generating this text as narrator and novelist. Grumm romanticizes childhood—after all, the title is *Portrait of a Romantic*—until he abruptly interrupts the speaker of such romantic sentiment with an explosion of hostility. Such sentimentality, Grumm implies, is an adult's sugar-coating of what the child knows as unrelieved boredom. Even now writing about his "massive Mommy" with her "bouncy cheeks" and "luscious red-brown hair" is boring enough to disrupt his song of himself.

Through Arthur Grumm, looking backward to his childhood, Millhauser is announcing the two faces of the Romantic sensibility. In his Whitmanesque opening, Grumm identifies himself as "lover and killer,"[5] who "sings" of "sunbeams and moonbeams," in an apostrophe to the "dark angels of my adolescence" (1). Those "dark angels" function as deliverers from the exquisite tedium of family life and school, only to play Russian roulette and join suicide clubs. That such playing with death was mere flirtation, however, is indicated by Grumm (a hybrid perhaps of "grim" and "glum") at twenty-nine having obviously survived adolescence.

These early chapters are reminiscent in other ways of Jeffrey's storytelling. Arthur also seems occasionally fetishistic about the details that call up memories of childhood. Even though he expresses horror at sentimentality, his endless cataloging of the boy's world expresses nostalgia for that boring childhood he attempts to dismiss. A case in point is his detailed description of a dozen or more specimens in his father's rock collection. The presence here of that great cataloger Walt Whitman suggests that Jeffrey and Arthur, perhaps Steven as well, share this American notion that things do not really exist until named, transforming fiction into archiving what might otherwise be lost. It is a variety of archeological study of the contemporary, as though the smallest of items in our everyday world are being treated as the historical specimens they may one day become.[6]

Portrait of a Romantic recalls *Edwin Mullhouse* in other ways. Like Jeffrey, Arthur is essentially a social isolate. Just as Jeffrey has no friends other than Edwin, Arthur seems friendless until he discovers his "double" in William Mainwaring, much as Edwin found his in Edward Penn. Unlike Penn, who just disappears, William eventually accepts Arthur's friendship and becomes one of the triads of Arthur's companions in adolescence. Ironically, as William is taken into the Grumm family and Arthur's parents clearly prefer him to their own son, the friendship of Arthur and William becomes ambivalent: part of Arthur understandably resents being supplanted by the "nice boy" William, who bores Arthur with his stamp collection, while a larger part of Arthur welcomes his friend's taking on "good-son," filial responsibility so that Arthur can enjoy the freedom of reverencing those "dark angels," leading him toward death.

On several levels, the summer Arthur is thirteen is the end of childhood. Like his cousin Marjorie, who is also thirteen, he is entering adolescence. The Marjorie of six who took the edge off summer's boredom when she introduced him to the game of 1–2-3, both-of-us-pull-down-our-pants, is now a "plain, dumpy, motherly sort of girl" (63), a female counterpart to William with whom Arthur plays endless games of Monopoly or ping-pong in the "dank shade" of the Grumm "cellar" (59), so different from Penn's "heated cellar" (*Edwin Mullhouse* 82). The "romantic" Arthur discloses his propensity for the "pathetic fallacy" of imputing human attributes to nature by opening a chapter with "The summer was bored to death. It sat with slack jaw and parted lips, gazing dully from beneath drooping eyelids" (59).

Arthur, some sixteen or so years later, may be accentuating that summer's boredom as a justification for his growing allegiance to the "dark angels," inciting him to dare increasingly dangerous rebellions against convention, as he moves more fully into adolescence. One episode of moon-mad hijinks seriously threatens the friendship with William. In the dead of night, Arthur enters the Mainwaring house with a key, "hidden" conventionally atop the doorframe, and gropes his way to William's bedroom. Even in the dark, Arthur surmises the startled William is "upset" at this "home invasion." When he discovers Arthur did it from his boredom-generated "moon-mood," William can scarcely contain his fury, fueled by anxiety that he might have to explain his friend's presence. Subsequently Arthur chooses not to explain to his own parents why William has not visited the Grumm house and retreats to his room to read most of the day. Readers of *Edwin Mullhouse* are justified in assuming the Grumms will never be visited by William again.

Some nights later, however, William returns. It is not when Arthur's parents are awake, however, but when the sleepless Arthur looks out his window to see William in the yard, illuminated by a "jaded moon, half dead with boredom" (78). William's entry through the kitchen window is a strange mixture of fantasy, or creative imagination, and actuality. At first Arthur describes William's movements as though he were narrating a novel in which his friend could replicate Arthur's break-in as a gesture of reconciliation. In actuality, Arthur apparently does see William at his bedroom door with "an expression of fierce triumph that mirrored" Arthur's. To Arthur, William's replication of Arthur's escapade brought "the bright beginning of a new intimacy" (80), an intimacy like Jeffrey and Edwin's once first Rose Dorn and then Arnold Hasselstrom are eliminated from the constellation of Edwin's friends.

Grumm's effort to accentuate the boredom of early adolescence reaches a climax in eighth grade, "that stifling grade" (85) when he committed his "mild crime" (89) of playing hooky to spend the day reading. Hindsight may be accentuating the boredom as the foundation of making new friends, the first of whom is Philip Schoolcraft, the "languid and dreamy" new student Arthur identifies not as his double but his "triple" (91). If Grumm begins his story with a pastiche of Walt Whitman's hearty "Song of Myself," embracing the totality of Life, Philip has constructed himself as a character out of Edgar Allan Poe's writing. This Prince of Poe in his darker, more melancholy and morbid realm is the epitome of boredom and lassitude, seeking perverse pleasures to escape the ennui of everyday ordinariness. Although Philip smokes cigarettes, readers expect him to move on to absinthe and opium, but they are apparently not yet readily available in small-town Connecticut a half-century ago.[7]

Ironically Philip's last name, "Schoolcraft," could not be less appropriate to his student demeanor. He turns in assignments regularly and then fails to. What infuriates his teachers even more is his refusal to offer even the lamest of excuses. Philip endears himself most to Arthur, however, by flagrantly failing to follow the assignment to memorize a poem from the assigned list and recite it in class. Instead Philip recites lines from Poe's story "The Masque of the Red Death" until his furious teacher stops his recitation, making it impossible for him to show off how much he had memorized.

Arthur, in turn as narrator, demonstrates his own memory of Philip's room when he visited it sixteen years earlier, enabling him to describe it in scrupulously complete detail. Philip seduces the naive Arthur by going beyond the decadence of Poe's writing to ask Arthur if he has ever read Robert Louis Stevenson's story "The Suicide Club," of which he "just happens" to recall having a second copy he could lend him, if Arthur will bring it from the bookshelf. Inside the book is a revolver, connecting Philip with Arnold Hasselstrom, who introduced Edwin to weapons. Eventually Philip demonstrates that he is the heir of nineteenth-century writers other than Poe and Stevenson. Herman Melville also appears to be a progenitor with his story "Bartleby the Scrivener," in which Bartleby eventually refuses to do any more copying of documents with his famous "I would prefer not to," and in his novel *The Confidence Man* in which Melville depicts the innocents of nineteenth-century America helpless before the predations of the adept "con-man," who delights in showing the naive their vulnerability in a world where some are not innocent.

The outcome of Philip's confidence game is the suicide pact he persuades Arthur to sign—in blood, of course. Arthur deludes himself into believing he and Philip have become "blood-brothers." When the date for their suicides arrives, Arthur begins to feel great tenderness toward his blood-brother, who he assumes must love him if he is willing to give his life to honor their agreement to die together. Adept confidence man that he is, Philip exposes his victim's naïveté by handing Arthur the revolver, handle first, completely undoing his victim's brotherly feelings by demonstrating that Arthur expected *Philip* to go first. Arthur is crushed by his brother's mocking disdain at his inability to fulfill his pledge, an inability that offers Philip an escape hatch from fulfilling *his* half of the suicide part. When Grumm rushes out, the friendship appears ended—at least temporarily. The latter is made possible by William's example of overcoming his anger at Arthur's "home invasion." Escaping to the boring but safe world of his friendship with William, Arthur will inevitably allow his boredom to prepare him for his next seducer.

This "seducer" is Arthur's classmate Eleanor whose long-term illness allows him the opportunity to deliver her assignments and collect her homework. If Philip's morbid preoccupation with death testifies to his citizenship in Poe country, Eleanor's alleged illness and physical frailty make her seem like a character right out of a Poe poem such as "Annabel Lee."[8] Arthur himself admits "secretly I called her The Phantom Eleanor" (148), in part because she appears in class after a long absence, only to be absent again for days, and even weeks. Additionally like women in Poe's world, Eleanor leaves the impression that her illness is not a symptom of weakness but an indication she is too good and pure to be in our fallen world.

Arthur's visit to Eleanor's house and her mother's offering easy access to her daughter's bedroom with no concerns about what could transpire there further locate this sequence of scenes in Poe country. Eleanor is too fragile, too "sisterly" for Arthur to have any designs on her sexually, any more than Poe had any base desire for his cousin and child-bride, the model for Annabel Lee. Although Eleanor is an adolescent, she is locked into a girl's asexual world of dolls and automatons, foreshadowing the later Millhauser stories "August Eschenburg" and "In the Penny Arcade."

Grumm describes one automaton in particular with an almost obsessive impulse to record its intricate motions. This clown figure juggles four differently colored balls, catching one after having thrown the next into the air. This description continues as though Arthur were in a trance, watching the clockwork movement of the figure and waiting perhaps for the number of balls to exceed the capacity of the mechanism to avoid dropping them. The sense of compulsive attention to the figure Grumm describes in an earlier self as "Arthur" is radically extended and intensified by the narrative's style. As the reader slowly becomes aware, not only do individual sentences run on and on, but this passage is all one long paragraph of eleven pages! Ultimately the inevitable happens when the clockwork figure can no longer keep up with the balls and they come crashing down. Eleanor's yanking the figure and saying, "How ugly!" brings to an end the spell the figure has cast on Arthur, and he is brought back to Eleanor's insistence that he must comment on this episode.

Arthur is exhausted and wants to go home, but Eleanor will have none of it. She scolds him for being a child and invites him into her inner sanctum, the Childhood Museum. This museum is a "large, many-windowed, mansion-like dollhouse" (183), in essence a miniature of the Schumann house, including Eleanor's room. We might go so far as to equate the Childhood Museum with Arthur's narrative, *Portrait of a Romantic,* for in many ways the young-adult Grumm is building a museum of his own childhood as he tells Arthur's story. The museum-dollhouse offers yet another opportunity for Grumm to describe in minute detail the contents of this miniaturized world. Additionally the Childhood Museum is an early expression of Millhauser's attraction to replicas and miniatures.

Although both Arthur and Eleanor are adolescents, they perform literary rituals we might expect of young children. They dress up in formal clothes to "marry," for example, without any suggestion of sexual content in this marriage ritual. Similarly, once again at Eleanor's instigation, they "die," stretched out on her bed, after having drunk an allegedly poisonous potion. Grumm actually states that Eleanor is planning the "drama of our death" (230). As in the suicide pact with Philip, there is no fear that Arthur will perish because he must survive to become Grumm the narrator. Within the logic of his narration, readers may ponder what exactly the adult Grumm is getting out of these childlike, repetitive performances. Is he intent on emphasizing the boredom of his "normal" life that drives him to such bizarre, but boring games? Or is Grumm dramatizing the preoccupation with death, especially self-inflicted death, being rehearsed as play before it becomes deadly serious, as in the games Jeffrey and Edwin play until Edwin ends up really dead?

Just when readers are likely to wonder how long these games will go on, Eleanor surprises Arthur on a visit in spring by showing signs of a "relentless recovery" (247). Grumm expresses something like nostalgia in his twisting of the sickness trope, asserting: "It was as if her illness were sick, and no longer had strength enough to resist the infection of health" (247). Eleanor has already torn down the heavy draperies to let in the light, and become a surprising dynamo of energy, intent on making up overdue assignments and writing papers to pass her courses. Eleanor's recovery will be played out again in "The Room in the Attic," when the narrator goes into a frenzy after Isabel allows light to violate her darkened room. Eventually Eleanor becomes so "busy" she no longer has time for him. Arthur, it would appear, has been feeding parasitically on her illness to avoid the ordinary world he finds so tedious. Like it or not, Arthur is being expelled from the Childhood Museum, back into the boring world of home and school—and of course William Mainwaring.

William has apparently undergone a transformation, however. The proviso of "apparently" is appropriate because like Jeffrey in *Edwin Mullhouse* Grumm has absolute control over the narrative. Following his replicating Arthur's home-invasion by secretly entering the Grumm house, William moves toward becoming Arthur's soul-mate, increasingly willing to experiment with Arthur's impulsive strategies to stave off boredom. After the dissolution of Arthur's friendship with Philip Schoolcraft and then again after the end of Arthur's "affair" with Eleanor Schumann,[9] William renews his function as the friend-of-last-resort, or perhaps as the embodiment of normalcy Arthur finds it gratifying to return to after his close encounter with death under Philip's tutelage and then his attraction to illness and depression under Eleanor's control. With his second return to normalcy, Arthur encounters a William who is a more tractable follower into the perverse pleasures of flirting with death Arthur learned from Philip's introduction to Russian roulette and suicide pacts. Perhaps to maintain Arthur's fidelity as a friend, William supplants Arthur in the games Arthur played with Philip. And unlike Arthur, William, to his own misfortune, is more seriously invested in playing Russian roulette with live ammunition.

The ending offers the culmination of the narrative's mixture of realism and surrealism. The final chapter begins with the realism that has dominated the narrative: "I closed the door softly behind me and for a few moments I stood leaning back against the door, listening to my heavy breathing and peering into opaque darkness" (309). In the split-second of visibility made possible by Arthur's flipping the light switch, some very select details are noted. With the return of darkness, however, the narrative changes into primarily dialogue, slowed down by the eventual absence of the identification of who is speaking. Then the expedient of lit matches allows for the cutting of a deck of cards, over and over, until William gets the ace of spades, marking him as the first to hold the revolver to his temple.

What follows is presumably the adult Grumm representing his younger-self Arthur's devolving into a breakdown of communication—and sanity. As in the even longer passage in the Eleanor section in which the narrative runs on as one extraordinarily long paragraph of almost a dozen pages, the ending becomes one long paragraph of sentences interrupted by ellipses, presumably to mark Arthur's mental breakdown under the guilty excitement of participating in William's risking his life to demonstrate his fidelity. Arthur persuades himself that this is all a dream, just as the narrative of William's entering the Grumm house to match Arthur's entry of the Mainwaring house has a dreamlike or surrealistic quality, leading the reader to wonder whether William was actually there or was merely a figment of Arthur's overheated imagination. Here, however, Arthur's "yes that's it, a dream, I'll wake up soon" is punctuated by the simple statement: "Somewhere a shot rang out" (316).

The rendering of this chaotic scene recalls the episode of Edwin Mullhouse's death, when Jeffrey impulsively "helps" his friend carry through on his pretense of taking his own life. Grumm as narrator adds another statement ending in an ellipsis: "And you, night voyager, my brother, my stranger: you too I sing, O dark romantic . . ." (316). Offering a bookend to the novel's Whitmanesque introduction, the assertion with its apostrophe to "my brother, my stranger" may momentarily appear to address the reader à la Baudelaire with the French poet's "you hypocrite reader, my twin, my brother." However, it is William Mainwaring who serves as the addressee of Grumm's long love letter, celebrating the boy he disdained as an inferior until William did what Arthur was not brave enough to do and thereby transformed himself into the true Romantic for whom this *Portrait* serves as monument.

CHAPTER 4

From the Realm of Morpheus

Steven Millhauser's third novel appeared almost a decade after *Portrait of a Romantic* (1986). As Danielle Alexander notes, Knopf offered to publish *From the Realm of Morpheus,* but only if the author was willing to make cuts in the manuscript, and Millhauser was unwilling. Although his dedication to his novel's integrity is commendable, Millhauser's decision was unfortunate because he missed the opportunity to have his third novel join his earlier two as publications of Knopf, highly regarded as a publisher of distinguished fiction. It was not until some years after he won the Pulitzer Prize for his next novel, *Martin Dressler,* that Knopf would renew its interest in his work, publishing *Dangerous Laughter* and then *We Others.*

After Millhauser shortened the manuscript, Morrow published *From the Realm of Morpheus* in 1986, the same year *In the Penny Arcade* appeared. The author subsequently admitted that his earlier attempt to publish the entire manuscript of a thousand-plus pages was an "error," adding that his decision to reduce the manuscript's length marked a "disenchantment with the aggression of length," which moved him toward "shorter forms."[1] In writing the original manuscript, Millhauser apparently joined his more imaginative characters in their frustration with their craft's conventions, impelling them to overreach—in a sense, to color outside the lines. The lack of critical response from book reviewers and academics was hardly surprising, since *From the Realm of Morpheus* challenges readers with its straining of the conventional notions of a novel.

In a limited sense of the term, *From the Realm of Morpheus* may be classified as a novel. Its sections, or "chapters," are held together by the narrator, a young American named Carl Hausman,[2] who sets the "plot" in motion when he pursues a baseball down into the Realm of Morpheus where he becomes the guest of Morpheus, the god of dreams. Like Dante telling his story of being led through the *Inferno* by Virgil, Carl tells his of exploring the subterranean "Realm" with Morpheus as guide. Carl's function as narrator limits his development as a character, turning him into the lens through which readers see Morpheus. If one convention of the novel is the expectation that its central figure(s) will change, that convention is held in abeyance. As a god, Morpheus presumably cannot actually "change," although he seems to. And the young mortal at the end seems little different from the Carl who entered the realm of Morpheus, rather like Alice falling down the rabbit hole.

From the Realm of Morpheus strains the conventions of the novel even more by being a conglomeration of short stories, or even novellas. These strains on the novel's conventions may lead readers to ask: Where is the sense of direction here? If the organizing principle seems almost "spatial," one section or story added to another, would it not be possible to rearrange the sections of *From the Realm of Morpheus* without any significant sense of difference? And more to the point of Millhauser's initial refusal to cut the extremely long manuscript, is it not possible to eliminate one or more sections of what amounts to a collection of shorter fiction, tied together through Carl, and Morpheus, who leads him through this "realm"? Would it change the work as a whole, for example, to excise the journey to the moon, which "ends" the book?

Several longer sections in *From the Realm of Morpheus* are important forerunners of Millhauser's later interest in the novella. This troublesome term "novella" has come into use as a means of denoting a narrative in the middle ground between the short story's restricted plot development and limited cast of characters, producing greater focus and compression, and the novel's expansiveness and ability to represent character change in a longer time span. Writers are frequently asked if they know at the outset whether the narrative they are writing will become a short story or a novel. Their usual response is that the narrative takes control and the author is less a puppeteer manipulating the story and more a stenographer taking it all down in haste, producing a short story or novella or novel as the narrative dictates. Despite the efforts to define these three forms as having qualitative differences, the matter usually comes down to page count.

Because most of the stories in *From the Realm of Morpheus* are "tales," they contain an element of ironic distancing. This distancing is a product of the tale's self-conscious departure from the "real world," carrying the reader into fantasy worlds, as exemplified by the "Arabian Nights." The tale also distinguishes itself from expressions of "realism" in its foregrounding of narrative as a *told* tale, heard by a figure in the tale, giving the sense of narration on which readers are eavesdropping. Basically the tale strategy balances the awareness that the tale is "just a story" and the reader's reliance on the teller and listener for the illusion of the tale's being "real."

Of the "novellas" in *From the Realm of Morpheus,* "The Tale of Ignotus," the "Unknown" one, is probably the most successful. Here the pastiche of Renaissance language, along with Byron's language, seems particularly appropriate because this story is heavily invested in the Renaissance theme of art vs. life. The melancholy story is generated by a young, fledgling artist's painting the picture of an Englishman, Lord Thomas Hall. The artist's mastery of verisimilitude is so successful that the portrait of the artist achieves the illusion of reality sought millennia ago by Roman painters who, in the classic example, could paint bunches of grapes so "real" that birds could be fooled into trying to eat them. As it later becomes clear, this painter, Felix Brendel, imbued the portrait of Lord Hall with his own romantic melancholy so powerfully that Hall, or "Ignotus," is a reflection of the artist's own youthful state. In a subtle twist of fantasy, the figure in the painting discovers his power to leave the two-dimensional, "dead" world of paint and canvas to become a living, breathing creature, unfortunately bearing his maker's melancholy as a fate shaping his existence back in the "real world" outside the painting.

Thus the painting becomes a portal through which Hall moves as he sits for his picture and out of which "Ignotus" eventually steps as the embodiment of the artist's melancholy. As a derivative, Byronic melancholic, Ignotus plays out his destiny by falling in love with the beautiful, sixteen-year-old Julia. After Julia's mother died, her dissolute father, the Margrave von Harnack, sent Julia to a convent to be "educated," but in actuality to preserve her chastity from men like himself. His Countess sister had all she could do to dissuade him from forcing Julia to become a nun and has now prevailed on her brother to allow his daughter to "come out" in society as a potential wife. When Julia meets and falls in love with Ignotus, her father is unhappy because this foreigner is no suitable match for his prized daughter. A cynic might question the lecherous father's motives, asking if he does not want to ensure that if he cannot have Julia no other man will.

Julia ups the ante by swearing she will marry Ignotus, or no one, promising to become a nun if her beloved betrays his vow to marry her. What Julia will never know is that Ignotus lives two lives. A seedy magician,[3] the "Great Stromboli," has discovered Ignotus's secret life in Brendel's painting and threatens to expose Ignotus if he refuses to perform his "magic trick" of stepping out of and back into the painting again and again. Stromboli alternately promises to eventually release his slave and threatens that his secret will be revealed should the magician be killed.

Much as readers may desire the promise to be kept, they sense it will be broken, as perhaps Ignotus does too. Our worse expectations become real when the betrothed lady loses faith in Ignotus, and although modern readers may prepare for the worst—her suicide—they forget the betrothed lady is a Christian for whom suicide is *the* unforgivable sin. Accordingly she does not take her own life but gives it to the Divine Bridegroom, consigning herself to a lifetime of waiting for her entry to Paradise. Ignotus may pound on the convent doors for all eternity, but his beloved has been sequestered from him and the temptations of the world. Like Byron's Childe Harold, Ignotus "trails the pageant of his bleeding heart" across Europe until he puts a bullet in his head and ends up in Morpheus's picture gallery.

A rival of this tale for the most successful "novella" in *Realm* is the story Morpheus tells Carl about his unsavory love life. Indeed feminists of earlier generations would likely have called Morpheus a "male chauvinist pig." "The Tale of Morpheus and Volumnia" offers an exemplum of the man who masquerades as a virtuous suitor and husband to please a "moral maid." This "maid" Volumnia was allegedly sired by a god and raised by a shepherd and his wife. After leading Morpheus on a merry chase by putting her foster sister Olympia in his way to test his "fidelity,"[4] this "moral maid" loses self-control, when a bee stings her, and impulsively gives herself to Morpheus. As in their married love to follow, Volumnia clearly enjoys sexual intercourse, even though she immediately returns to her masquerade of moral disdain for connubial love.

The tale turns nasty after Volumnia brings a couple of servants into the household. The nastiness is generated by these servants, who are married dwarves,[5] chosen by Volumnia as a solution to the predatory nature of the lustful Morpheus, who surmises his wife believes he will be put off by an ugly, married dwarf. Morpheus proves her wrong by taking Rosabella as his mistress and delighting in the company of her husband Scurlock, who titillates him by describing Rosabella's sexual cravings, and later develops a "cash-flow" problem once he has become his wife's procurer.

Essentially the "nastiness" has its source in the traditional perverse fascination with dwarves, kept at royal and ducal courts as amusements for those who, like Morpheus, took perverse pleasure in fantasizing about the dwarf as a sexual partner, just as they might imagine having sex with someone of a different race or species. In the end Morpheus discovers that he has been victim of a clever ruse. While he was having sex with Rosabella, the virtuous Volumnia was in bed with Scurlock. After being discovered *in flagrante delicto,* Volumnia compounds the story's nastiness by bringing her foster sister, Olympia, into bed with Morpheus on one side of Volumnia and Olympia on the other. When she concludes they are asleep, Volumnia quietly leaves the bed, expecting the two to awaken and make love. Morpheus *says* he steeled himself to resist temptation, but it is *his* story, whose thesis is: never marry a virtuous woman. Hoping to halt Volumnia's efforts to debauch Olympia, Morpheus eventually confesses his adultery with Rosabella. It is to no avail, however, because Volumnia, who will later bear a son, leaves Morpheus to set up housekeeping with Olympia.

The unpleasantness of Morpheus's tale may be even greater than initially meets the eye. As teller of this tale, Morpheus may have censored the distinct possibility that the father of Volumnia's son is Scurlock, not Morpheus. Given his withholding the truth of his adultery with Rosabella, Morpheus may be suppressing his suspicion that he is sterile. Within the dynamic of narration, what Morpheus says is influenced by his audience of one—the young, naive Carl. Additionally the cynical reader may surmise that Volumnia was involved with Scurlock before she brought the couple into the household, knowing full well that her husband was so lecherous he would be attracted to "even" a dwarf. His lust is aroused in part by her size: Rosabella is the height of a pre-teen, and yet she is a woman. Because Morpheus himself is telling this perverse tale, the narrative lacks the saving grace of irony to distance readers from the perverse attitudes toward dwarves in the Renaissance, associated with Morpheus's imitation of that period's language.

Like "The Tale of Morpheus and Volumnia," yet another novella-length tale which might challenge the complexity of "Ignotus" is "The Tale of Heklo and Ekli," also a tale of an impossible love relationship. This tale focuses on the brother and sister giants whom Carl and Morpheus visit in the latter's "Realm." In "Heklo and Ekli" it is the presumably virginal Carl who tells a tale at whose center is the pathos of his relationship with the giantess Ekli. One major factor in his affection for Ekli is the sad episode of her having fallen in love, years earlier, with Heklo's giant poet-friend, who abruptly abandoned her, writing a farewell letter to her brother but none to her. Yet another factor is the difference in size between Ekli and Carl, recalling Jonathan Swift's Brobdingnagians, whose huge size miniaturizes Gulliver, as their immensity calls up images for him of their grossness. Here, however, the comic element is generally suppressed, except in Morpheus's lectures on the lustfulness of giantesses and his own success in love-making with a giantess, for whom he must have seemed a very little boy.

Carl considers marrying Ekli, for whom he feels "tenderness." In his innocence about romantic or sexual relations, Carl has difficulty figuring out how to respond to a sensitive, loving woman who is also a giant. Even reading the narrative, rather than watching it as film, makes it difficult to respond sympathetically as he strokes first her finger, then her breast. Indeed the relationship would be much easier to render as comedy than pathos in which we are reminded of how loving another in a social context is fraught with pain when the couple does not fit into our notions of how they should look together, or more generally speaking how much our estimates of people depend on appearance.

If any of his experiences qualifies Carl for growth as a fictional character, it is probably his extended relationship with a woman who is about five times his size. Carl demonstrates his movement toward manhood by his "courage" in exposing his "tenderness," to borrow Lady Chatterley's high praise for her Lover. His quite innocent affection for Ekli is dramatically emphasized by Morpheus's greater experience and more predatory sexuality. Although Carl says nothing about it, he at least senses the cruel truth that size really does matter and he cannot envision a life with a wife who could crush him if she rolled over in bed. In the end he abandons her as her first lover did, and once again Heklo will be forced to minister to his sister's grief in being abandoned by a man she fell in love with.

It is hardly a coincidence that the other Morpheus tale follows the "Tale of Heklo and Ekli," for "The Tale of Morpheus and Vivayne" is also a story of an impossible love, surprising because the lover is Morpheus. The tale may not seem to fit the teller, as is often the case in Chaucer's *Canterbury Tales*, an obvious analog for this novel; this is, however, earlier in Morpheus's life (perhaps the gods change too!). He begins: "'Twas in my wenching days, long before I met wi' virtue'" (*From the Realm of Morpheus* 258), that is, Volumnia. Among the "'sea-lasses'" with whom he "'dallied,'" Illore particularly aroused his desire to go beyond "'boyish clips [hugs] and kisses'" to "'have the plunging pleasure too'" (259). Somehow his lust urged him to find the means to imitate "'the ways o' forked love,'" not elucidated by the teller, that could "'enflame and madden'" him enough to make "'true-forked love'" seem by comparison tame (259), and get Illore expelled from the school of maidens. Her expulsion might seem to make her Morpheus's slave, but he becomes her "'thrall,'" not so much because of her Venus-like "'upper half'" as her "'nether part,'" which can rouse his "'long-dulled senses wi' sharp delight'" (260). Thus this tale explores yet another facet of the teller's perverse sexuality in somehow coupling with a female who is half-fish.

Like the other story Morpheus told of his love life, "The Tale of Morpheus and Vivayne" becomes a story of Morpheus and two women. Soon after Illore and Morpheus move toward independent living, they meet one of the "'old girls,'" a young maiden mermaid named Vivayne, who is still "in school" and presumably virginal because never touched by a merman, or even a "merboy." When Morpheus finds that Vivayne has alienated Illore's affections and made him "'feel the lecher,'" he begins to hate this intruder who has made him feel the "odd man out." After Vivayne goes away, however, first Illore and then Morpheus discover he loves Vivayne. Illore loves him so much that she asks Vivayne to rejoin them and relieve Morpheus's pangs of unrequited love. However, Vivayne is so appalled at being seen by Morpheus that she threatens to poke her eyes out or set herself on fire. Morpheus invades her cave, but Vivayne escapes, leaving Morpheus waiting in vain for her return and unable to face Illore, whom he has caused such pain that she dies of a broken heart.

Also in *From the Realm of Morpheus* are the novella-length "Tale of the City in the Sea," an Atlantis in which everything is humanly constructed, even clouds and the sky, and "The Tale of a Voyage to the Moon."[6] Neither has the power of "A Tale of Ignotus." Two other sections fill out this "novel." "Mirror Tales" makes a gesture toward narrative, but the section is grounded in the extended exploration of the supposition that a mirror can take on an existence of its own.

Finally "The Library of Morpheus" makes no pretense to being a tale, although it offers a fascinating take on a "library" none of us has ever entered, although many might wish to. Shelved in Morpheus's library are all the unfinished works such as *The Canterbury Tales, Kubla Khan,* and *Don Juan,* now completed by Chaucer, Coleridge, and Byron, respectively. Elsewhere his library contains, according to Morpheus, "'all the lost books o' th'ancient world'" such as "'the hundred lost plays of Sophocles,'" as well as "'the complete collections once housed in the lost libraries of Alexandria and Pergamum'" (126, 128). Then the narrative moves toward an overreaching by exploring a section of books that might have been written but were not "'i' th'upper world,'" such as the novel after Joyce's *Finnegans Wake* or the play after *The Tempest* (130). Another section contains more fantastic books such as huge books written in "Brobdingnagian," the language of Swift's giants. The narrative continues pushing the envelope to include books debating each other's relative merit and eventually characters stepping out of their individual books and conversing with each other, such as Catherine Earnshaw from *Wuthering Heights* talking to Leopold Bloom from *Ulysses.* Although not a "tale," this section has a whimsical rendition of an English major's fantasy of what a library might be.

Millhauser's struggle to bring his manuscript into line with the length publishers prefer and the less than overwhelming response when *From the*

Realm of Morpheus was first published have encouraged him to feel protective of this novel and quickly come to its defense. After *From the Realm of Morpheus* he focused on short stories and novellas, and it was not until he was writing "Paradise Park" that some elements of Sarabee had the potential to generate a novel, encouraging him to set them aside and return to them in writing his novel *Martin Dressler.*

CHAPTER 5

In the Penny Arcade

After the high expectations generated by his first novel, *Edwin Mullhouse,* the second novel, *Portrait of a Romantic* (1977), was less well received. Although it might be understandable if he had some doubts about continuing in that genre, Millhauser spent almost a decade working on his third novel, *In the Realm of Morpheus,* a manuscript that eventually ran over a thousand pages. Three years into his work on *In the Realm of Morpheus,* as he indicates, he gave himself "permission" to write a story, one of the two he published in the *New Yorker* in the early 1980s—"A Protest Against the Sun" (1981) and "The Sledding Party" (1982). These two stories joined "A Day in the Country" to form the triad of realist stories in *In the Penny Arcade* (1986). He has said that they appeared in his first collection as a gesture of farewell to a mode in which he did not expect to write again. With their departures into fantasy, the last three stories—"Snowmen," the title story "In the Penny Arcade," and "Cathay"—are substantially different from the stories in "Part II" and much more like Millhauser's second and third novels.

If the three stories in "Part II" fit together because they have their roots in conventional realism and the three stories in "Part III" generate dynamic tension to "Part II," with their flights of fancy, "August Eschenburg," originally published by *Antaeus* in 1983, provides a strong introduction to the collection by balancing realism and fantasy. "August Eschenburg" recalls Millhauser's first novel, in which Jeffrey, the embodiment of obsessive preoccupation with details, was balanced by Edwin and the fantasy elements of his creative productivity in *Cartoons.* As an artist/technician, August combines obsessive attention to the details of automaton-making with the fantasy elements in his increasingly complex replications of human movement. Millhauser produces a realistically believable world, then subtly moves into a fantasy world readers accept as a logical extension. Eventually, however, they find themselves asking, Is August's "mad" pursuit of his art in ever-more life-like automatons technologically possible? The question is delayed, however, by the narrative's careful engineering of the transition into feats of August's ever-more complex artistry.

The connection between realism and fantasy is established at the very outset of "August Eschenburg" by Millhauser's strategic decision to begin with a series of events, determining August's future as an automaton-maker. When August is eight, he encounters one after another "cruel and marvelous toy" (*In the Penny Arcade* 3) in a field where he plays. Each toy is "cruel" because boys have put a bird inside a paper figure to enjoy watching its desperate struggles to escape. At eight, August knows his watching the bird suffer is wrong, but he is irresistibly attracted to this "marvelous toy" (3), not for sadistic pleasure at the bird's struggles but to marvel at how those struggles animate the figure. Even after the paper figures "mysteriously" disappeared, "he never forgot the sense of fear and wonder" (4) they produced. Presumably the "fear" is generated by his sense of potential punishment for his violation of life in his ever-more sophisticated efforts at producing a machine that seduces the viewer into believing the automaton is alive. We might recall the ancient Hebrew commandment against "graven images," based on the precept that creativity ought to be the sole domain of the Creator.

These animated figures are related to the wind-up, or "clockwork," toys for which he had developed a fondness, and it is no coincidence his father makes and repairs watches and clocks. Another formative experience is his father's showing him the workings of a watch. He may be unable to follow his father's explanation, but he marvels at the mystery of how the wheels move the watch's hands. The connection of this formative experience with the earlier one is confirmed by August's pleasure in holding a watch and feeling its "secret mechanism beating inside like the heart of a bird" (4). Motion becomes so synonymous with interconnected wheels that when his father takes him to the beach August is "hurt by his father's gentle laugh when he asked whether the waves had wheels inside" (4).

Other formative experiences abound for the boy August. He was so young when his mother died that he knows her only as a "shadow" in a framed silhouette. Because his father never forgives himself for not having his wife's photograph taken to remember her by, he makes sure August's photograph is taken. It is a marvel to the boy, given that photography was a "new art" (6). This experience is connected to the father and son's visit to an art museum whose paintings bore August because they all look the same. Boredom gives way to excitement, however, when his father finds a guard to show them a "magic picture," whose objects fantastically "move." Employing his knowledge of clockwork, August, now twelve, sets about constructing a moving picture of his own.

The combination of these formative experiences—the dead mother's unsatisfying shadow in the silhouette giving way to the superior photograph and in turn the "moving picture" supplanting the oil painting—offers a rendition of graphic technology challenging and bettering traditional art as expressions of what the eye perceives. The narrator interrupts the progression of August's artistic development to offer a "flash-forward" so that these formative experiences function as a fate controlling his life. This strategy offers depth by exposing the older August, seeking a pattern in his life, and focusing on these moments "after which nothing would ever be the same" (8).

One such moment happens to August in early adolescence when his father takes him to a fair for his fourteenth birthday. Like the jaded attitude of the boy in the later story "In the Penny Arcade," August's earlier excitement with the fair has turned to disappointment. After being annoyed by simple magic tricks for children in the "dark green tent" of "KONRAD THE MAGICIAN," he pays attention to the illusionist's announcement that he will shrink himself to perform in a small box. The tricks performed by a magician several inches tall amuse August, but it is the automaton itself that fascinates him with its "smooth and lifelike motions" (12). From the viewpoint of a future, knowing August, the episode is transformative: "To those few minutes in a drab green tent, August ever after traced his devotion to clockwork art" (13).[1]

The remainder of the first section, "Young Eschenburg," is devoted to his learning how to construct not a "clockwork toy," but "clockwork art" (13).[2] By his later teens August has become proficient enough in his art to attract the admiring gaze of villagers after he decides to improve his father's fortunes by displaying his clockwork figures in the shop window, as young Martin Dressler will construct a cigar tree in his father's tobacco-shop window. Success, however, makes August "secretly uneasy," because this "business part of things was a mysterious and amusing accident that had nothing to do with clockwork . . . and someday he would be exposed as a dreamer, a ne'er-do-well, a seedy magician in a drab green tent" (16–17). Soon his anxiety is greatly increased when his art attracts the attention of "Herr Preisendanz," who offers August an irresistible signing package to come to his Berlin department store and create clockwork figures to lure shoppers.

August's father Joseph is pivotal in the decision to accept the offer. The death of his wife has reconstructed Joseph as mother/father, supporting August's pursuit of artistic/socio-economic advancement. Another father might have resented August's mastery of clockwork or wanted to keep him as an assistant, sharing his menial labors and easing that burden in old age. But Joseph knows his son has a "gift" and deserves a "chance," which "might never come again" (18). At first, all goes disturbingly well: August savors the delight of being able to devote all his waking hours to his art, even spending his nights in his workshop.[3]

Eventually August's automatons both succeed in attracting customers and fail when the Preisendanz Emporium loses customers to his competition, the "Grimm Brothers." The automatons of the Grimms have a greater appeal to Berliners, who enjoy the "naughty" eroticism involving very young girls. When August refuses to pervert his art for money, Preisendanz terminates him. With August's return to his father's shop, Part II ends with August beginning a two-year period as his father's assistant, impatient with the lost hours to make automatons.

In Part III, "The Magic Theater," August eventually learns that Preisendanz hired the successful automaton-maker away from the Grimms. This automaton-maker is "Hausenstein," who cynically panders to the depraved taste of what he calls "the Untermenschen," or inferior people, a play on Friedrich Nietzsche's Übermensch, or "superman." Hausenstein lures August back to Berlin by providing him with a "Magic Theater" in which to perform his artistic mastery. Because Hausenstein represents the aspect of nineteenth-century technology whose sole motivation is profit-making, he attempts to undermine August's dedication to perfecting the technology of automaton-making as an art, that is, for aesthetic purposes. To Hausenstein, automaton-making was merely a primitive effort to represent the magic of motion as a precursor to filmmaking. To August, the craft of automaton-making may have begun as a means of supporting the automaton-maker's livelihood, but it became an art. Eventually filmmaking would reveal a similar conflict between "Hollywood," or using film technology for profit, and the later concept of film as an art-form, just as the earlier notion of photography's purpose as merely "taking pictures," or recording what the camera eye sees to transmit to others not present, would give way to the concept of the photograph as a potential work of art, like the watercolor or oil painting. Hausenstein can admire August's automatons, but only as quaint antiques, like nineteenth-century "flip books."

Hausenstein becomes central to the novella's development of August's tragedy. If August is impelled by the sacred pursuit of art for its own sake, Hausenstein is a Satan-figure who lures him back to Berlin for a far more devastating disillusionment than Preisendanz's firing him. When Hausenstein sets up the "Magic Theater," August is being set up by his Tempter to immerse himself all the deeper in what Hausenstein will ultimately identify as his victim's illusion of an audience for a pure art of automatons. Hausenstein will force August to confront the spirit of the "Untermensch," not the "overman" of Nietzsche, but the "underman," synonymous with modernity, a "soul that, in the presence of anything great, or noble, or beautiful, or original, instinctively longed to pull it down and reduce it to a common level" (35).

August's Magic Theater initially succeeds in drawing audiences into the illusion that it is humans, not automatons, they are watching. Some viewers return again and again to experience the same performances, and Hausenstein commends August's figures as among the "greatest automatons" in the last century and a half. Indeed August has transcended the technical accomplishments of his predecessors in his continuing pursuit of perfectly replicating the "motions of human musculature" (38). The pursuit is "madness," says Hausenstein, yet "as good a way as another to pass the time" (38).[4] But inevitably the audiences dwindle, and August discovers he has competition.

Eventually Hausenstein takes August to the competing theater, "At the Sign of the Black Boot." There he sees his competition fulfilling the Untermensch's needs by offering automaton performances of gross sexual acts, the precursors of "live sex shows" in our time. Eventually Hausenstein discloses that he established this theater not only for financial gain but to demonstrate to his "gifted but oh so innocent friend" that "automatons are dead" and that only perverse uses will keep them around as lewd antiques. After being disillusioned at sixteen by the married woman he loved, when she revealed that love and art for her were the facade of depravity and bestiality, Hausenstein knows the Untermenschen so well that he has become their Prince.

Once again August turns homeward, or to Mühlenberg, with the few automatons his suitcase can hold. Resting in the countryside while waiting for the coach, he ponders the large questions of what life is, in what Millhauser produces as a bravura performance of a middle-aged man assessing his life: "One day his father had opened the back of a watch and shown him the wheels inside. Was that his life? A bird inside a funny paper man, the boats in the picture that suddenly began to move, a perspiring magician in a drab green tent—were these the secret signs of a destiny . . . Or were they merely accidents, chosen by memory among the many accidents that constitute a life?" (64). To some readers the scene discloses the dreaded nightmare of looking back and asking: What is a life? with its corollary, Has any of it been worth the effort? Exhausted by the recognition that he has allowed what he despairingly terms a "childish passion" to consume his youth, whose loss he grieves, he falls asleep and awakens to the fear that even his suitcase has been stolen. Finding it boosts his spirits, however. He will not be defeated. He will create his automatons, despite the loss of audiences, because creating itself is ultimately the value of art. Having grown to admire August, readers feel the immense pain of his disillusionment, especially in his questioning: has my art, my life's work, been anything but the child's play of the self-deluded, especially in a age where success is pandering to the basest desires of the lowest common denominator?[5]

Millhauser has indicated that the stories in Part II—"A Protest Against the Sun," "The Sledding Party," and "A Day in the Country"—have a special purpose in this first collection of his stories. He included them as "a way of saying farewell to those middle stories, which I knew I would never return to, and also honoring them in a sense."[6] The three stories form a coherent group because they have much in common. They are all written in a realist style, two of the three originally appearing in the *New Yorker.* Each is set in the present and in the United States, rather than August's Germany of a century ago. Each has a female viewpoint character, in contrast to his other stories and his novels where that function is male.

Like the viewpoint characters in the other two stories, Elizabeth in "A Protest Against the Sun" seems socially insecure. Although she is a young adult, she has come to the beach with her parents and seems to enjoy continuing the little jokes and games from her childhood. Her child position causes some uneasiness, and she makes a point of reminding herself she is no longer a virgin, almost as though she is self-conscious of the reader's amusement or even disdain at her being here with family rather than friends her own age. This lack of ease, perhaps even embarrassment in being with her family, surfaces when she shares the "protest" of the sixteen-year-old boy in dark clothes and a hooded parka, as he tramps around the beach in disdain of others enjoying the sun. Although Elizabeth may not notice it, the boy is described as having "dark-tanned cheeks" (76), suggesting he may have to work in the sun that these beach-goers opt for to get a tan.

One source of difficulty is the indeterminacy of her age. The narrative indicates the time setting as "late August," and "she would soon be away at school again" (71). In an academic context—the father is a professor—Millhauser would expect "school" to denote "college." After all, she makes a point of not being a virgin, but readers are likely to assume she is in high school, where many young women today are no longer virgins. The intrusion of the boy in the black, hooded outfit may well impel her toward recognizing how alone in the world she is and how attractive she finds the warmth and security of childhood. Readers may miss the epiphany, however, as they are less likely to in the title story, "In the Penny Arcade," and presume that Elizabeth is sixteen or seventeen, rather than some years older, as the author intends. Her addressing her father as "Daddy" may assure readers they were right in guessing Elizabeth is a teenager, rather than a young woman impelled back toward family ties by the protestor's aloneness, as it encouraged her to recognize her own.

Catherine in "The Sledding Party" is a loner, young and self-immersed. She appears relieved to get away from the party to join the sledding. Perhaps the other young women's criticism of Sonia Holmes for coming to the party in a skirt and nylons threatens Catherine's security by making her wonder what they will say about *her* when she is absent. Soon she is sledding with Peter, who takes the opportunity to whisper "Love you." Rather than being pleased by his expression of love, she is disconcerted: "She felt violated, betrayed" (86). In the remainder of the story, she analyzes her sense that Peter has violated or betrayed her understanding of the relationship as comradeship rather than a potential romance. Catherine likens the words Peter whispered in her ear to a physical violation: it was as though "he had suddenly touched her breast" (90). Gradually she relinquishes her older, more innocent, even virginal notion that falling in love would involve some mysterious stranger in some other world and supplants that fantasy with the knowledge that love can occur between two friends or comrades.[7] In the process Catherine begins to lift herself from childlike self-immersion onto a plane where adult love can happen.

Judith, the viewpoint character in the last story of this trio, has taken time off from her job as an editor to spend "A Day in the Country." She is clearly the most mature of the three viewpoint characters; indeed, at thirty-six she is almost the ages of Elizabeth and Catherine combined. Even so, she is ill at ease, especially because of the "woman with melancholy eyes and a mane of black hair" (102), whose pity feels like a violation of her privacy. Judith is particularly exposed, or vulnerable, because she has looked enviously at the young lovers on blankets at the cliff's edge; then at dinner an older couple invited her to join them after seeing her "all by her lonesome" (111).

Although exhausted by her hike and even more by being forced to confront personal issues she avoided at her job, Judith cannot sleep and encounters the woman who pities her when she goes down to the library for a book. The woman tells Judith that when they met earlier she was sure Judith wanted to speak to her because Judith looks "so unhappy" (115). Offended by this exposure of her vulnerability, Judith coldly rejects the woman's overture and rushes "violently" to her room, where she collapses in uncontrollable weeping. She weeps for herself because of a failed relationship with a "beautiful weak man," but eventually more generously for the young lovers, oblivious of sorrow awaiting them, for the older couple awaking at night with "death fear," but also for the "dark woman, who in the arrogance of her sadness had developed cruel gifts of divination" (117). In the moonlight Judith returns to the cliff, causing the reader anxiety that she is suicidal, but she tells herself, "It's over now" (121). Through the dark woman's agency, Judith has come through the darkness with the strength to go on.

The three stories that comprise Part III of *In the Penny Arcade* transport this collection well into the world of the imagination and fantasy. The third story—"Cathay"—is the least like the other stories of this collection. It is clearly a fable, set in an "other" world, indicated by its title, the romantic term for China. The first two stories—"Snowmen" and "In the Penny Arcade"—have ties with the Part II stories because they are definitely set in contemporary America. Both have young, male viewpoint characters, connecting them with the earliest chapters of "August Eschenburg." Like that novella, these two stories begin well-grounded in the real world before they move into fantasy. That movement is justified, however, by the narrative function of the boys. As first-person narrator, each boy encourages us to accept the fantasy elements as natural extensions of the narrator's highly imaginative, youthful excitement with life. If the narrator of the title story initially performs the conventional adolescent boy's blasé, bored response to what thrilled the child who used to be excited by the arcade, the ending testifies to the potential to regain the paradise lost of the child's enthusiasm.

The opening of "Snowmen" offers another illustration of how useful first-person narrators are to stories of imagination and fantasy. Because the boy is totally immersed in his world, he provides few of the "facts" readers would expect in third-person narrative. He names his playmates—all boys—who join him in making snowmen, but he omits his own name, along with his age, his family, his geographical location, plainly because *he* knows all that. Besides, he is telling this story on the principle that the sheer excitement of the snow-sculpting is what's important, and this experience excludes awareness of his narrative as a story with an audience. Also because the unnamed boy is telling a story whose action is already completed, the effects of its ending are apparent at the outset.

"Snowmen" launches readers immediately into the intense excitement of children's awaking to an immense snowfall. Since his world has been transformed without warning, the boy-narrator easily transmits the notion of a magical, fantasy world of snowdrifts like sea waves, as though a sorcerer had waved a magic wand. The wild, furious delight in the energy that reshaped his world infects the boy and his playmates with the contagion of excitement that has the power to transform the ordinary into the fantastic. The process is marked by the initial description of children making snow*men,* even though some represent women and children—no political correctness in these boys' world. Soon, however, the clumsy snow figures most readers have made as children metamorphose into incredibly intricate and complicated snow sculptures that even adults could not conceive of making, much less of creating.

The boy-narrator speculates that a single "child of genius, maddened and inspired by our fervent snow," instigated the frenzy of snow-sculpting, copied by the others who competed among themselves to transcend what had been created. The subtext seems to be Shakespeare's line that "the lunatic, the lover, and the poet are of imagination all compact." The context of dazzling snow in winter sunshine only adds to the conventional wisdom of snow madness. The second-day activities of the children are dominated by a frenzy of feverish creativity that moves over into a fantasy, not immediately noticed because the narrator is immersed in the snow-sculpting he describes.

The high level of refinement in representing trees and animals in snow transforms these pre-adolescent children into Michelangelos of snow-sculpting. The narrator's description is so replete with realistic detail, rendered with such minute technical mastery, that readers may find themselves wanting to believe in this "fantastic" art, until they are jolted by descriptions of snow-sculptures that *have* to be fantasies because not even adults could sculpt them. One example will suffice: trees made of snow, we are asked to believe, are "composed leaf by leaf, with visible veins" (130). Almost aware that these descriptions seem a hoax, the narrator himself foregrounds the implausibility of the snow sculptures as "showing evidence of a skill so excessive, an elaboration so painfully and exquisitely minute, that it could scarcely conceal a desperate restlessness" (130).

That "restlessness" speaks to something intrinsic to the world according to Millhauser. We have seen it in *Edwin Mullhouse* and "August Eschenburg," and will see it repeatedly in his fiction. Basically it is the sentiment that genius is no more than the ability/willingness to follow our obsessions, as children do until any genius they may have had is eradicated by conditioning. Given that children are prescient enough to foresee its absence in adults' boredom and conformity, Millhauser's children frequently follow their obsessions with manic self-abandon—before it's too late. As the children-sculptors sense, creativity can produce a mania and—as we see in the second novel, *Portrait of a Romantic*—a corresponding depression, with suicidal dimensions when the boredom of the adult world can be faced only through the excitement of, say, "Russian roulette." In "Snowmen" the boy-narrator speaks for the others' happiness when the winter thaw seems nature's way of restoring balance, and for a time at least the familiar sounds of winter boots scuffing on pavement can be welcome antidotes to the "leaping ballerinas and prancing clowns" (132) of their snow-art.

The title story, "In the Penny Arcade," recalls the modernist tradition of writers such as James Joyce, whose focus was occasionally children on the brink of adolescence, experiencing a moment of recognition, or to use Joyce's trope, an "epiphany."[8] Millhauser's boy-narrator economically sets the scene: at twelve he has left his parents waiting on the "green bench beside the brilliant white ticket booth" (135) in the August sunshine to enter the darkness of the arcade. He is reporting that he is a "big boy now," returning after two years, when his parents might have accompanied him. He has "dreamed of" this visit "that tense, enigmatic summer, when the world seemed hushed and expectant, as if on the verge of revealing an overwhelming secret" (135).

Along with the dreaming, there has also been dread, foreshadowed by his disappointment that the darkness inside is not dark enough. From his viewpoint the question is: will this return end in disappointment because the *arcade,* not he, might have changed? Readers of *Edwin Mullhouse* may recall Jeffrey's almost traumatic experience of returning to White Beach with Edwin and being appalled at its reflection of their inner transformation to come. The narrator's loss of innocence surfaces here in the fortuneteller automaton, which has "aged": one eye has "nearly faded away," a finger is "chipped," her nose is cracked, but what's worse, boredom has "withered her spirit" (136, 137). The Queen of the Penny Arcade has lost all her otherworldly power to enchant.

And the contagion of age has spread to the other figures. More significant is the cowboy figure with which the narrator once had to *struggle* to match the quickness of the cowboy's draw for only a dime. Now the gunslinger speaks so slowly that the boy has shot him before the automaton has finished his challenge to draw. Even the "half-naked woman" performing a circus act on horseback has become pathetically old and dusty to his eyes, as he peers through a peepshow window. She seems the most disappointing of these decrepit figures because he had expected "some unspoken promise to be fulfilled" (139). The modifier "half-naked" suggests that the "unspoken promise" the boy anticipated is the mystery of sexuality to be revealed by her becoming more than "*half*-naked." Readers may suspect that the narrator subconsciously postponed this return until at twelve he now feels old enough for her to uncover her hidden mysteries.

This reading is supported after the boy has discovered what he believes is the "true" arcade figures in an alcove, concealed by darkness from the view of other visitors, who see only the "impostors" of these true figures he recalls from childhood. This passage requires extremely careful attention, or the reader may easily become confused. The boy indicates that he "stepped over the rope and entered the forbidden darkness" where the power of his desire to recuperate the figures as his innocent eyes perceived them now leads him to *imagine* them, even though he cannot see them in the darkness. It is the force of his imagination that posits the presence of these unseen figures, and the strength of first-person narrative, earlier grounded in the reality of the arcade as he now sees it, that can lead readers astray, that is, into believing there are actually two sets of figures in the arcade, rather than just one, which he saw as a child, as a blasé early adolescent, and eventually as a young adult who has recuperated his capacity to see again through more innocent eyes. The cue readers must not miss is his departure from the "dark alcove" where memory and desire allow him to re-view the figures: "I hurried to the rope and stepped into safety" (140). It is a "safety" suggesting that he must recover the power to see as a child, not retreat to childhood from the complexity of adult experience.

Through the innocent child's eyes he can once again recover the arcade figures, brought back to life. The narrator and the reader can see it in their powerful eyes: the cowboy's "eyes blazed darkly," while the fortuneteller now stares "with piercing blue eyes" (141). And it is no coincidence that the third figure he turns to is the circus performer. Renewed by the gunslinger's recovered potency, and the boy's "excitement," her earlier promise of a "revelation" is indicated by the narrator's elided referencing of her as "the woman" he sees when he "pressed [his] hot forehead onto the cool metal" (142). This time she exposes exactly what he had been hoping to see: after she dismounts her horse and enters her bedroom, she takes off most of her clothes. "I had the sense that I was coming closer and closer to a dark mystery that cunningly eluded me" (143). Given that the boy is no longer the ten-year-old of his earlier visit when he saw nothing, the narrator has been gazing and reading about the "dark mystery" of women.[9] The woman's leading him "into a lush and intricate realm of always more dangerous exposures which themselves proved to be new and dazzling concealments" moves toward its climax, but is interrupted by a boy's shouting.

The consequences of this striptease fantasy are fruitful, however, despite the interruption that yanks the boy back into the "real world." There he enunciates the "secret," the revelation, or "epiphany" stimulated by the woman's disrobing.[10] Because the narrative is first-person, Millhauser justifies the boy's spelling out his epiphany. Like Beauty, Truth is in the eye of the beholder. The arcade had become a collection of junk because the visitors had lost the power of their innocent viewing. The boy reveals his own culpability in joining the "conspiracy of dullness." The figures have not betrayed him; he has betrayed *them* by falling prey to the "ordinary." He steps "decisively" from the arcade's enlightening darkness into the "dazzle" of the late-summer sun, where he promises to remain "vigilant" in avoiding the perceptions of the ordinary.

Because "In the Penny Arcade" is a modernist story, it would have been tempting for Millhauser to have positioned *it,* not "Cathay," last in the collection. Unlike "Arcade" with its tight structure, "Cathay" is a loose grouping of vignettes of varying length. Although obviously prose, not poetry, the extremely brief section "Blue Horses," for example, is reminiscent of haiku in its highly compressed, imagistic qualities: "The Emperor's blue horses in a field of white snow" (160). As a whole and in its sections, this "story" lacks anything resembling a plot, except for the final section, which could stand alone as a fable. Then again, "Cathay" as a collection might be called a "fable," with the last section providing its "moral."

The end position of "Cathay" is justified by its sharing with the opening novella several themes and issues that bookend the intervening stories. Like "August Eschenburg," "Cathay" is set in an "other," older culture, indeed a culture that seems timeless, even though its Emperor is obsessed with hourglasses. More explicitly than "August Eschenburg," "Cathay" reveals an obsession with miniatures. Additionally, although some of the intervening stories are concerned with art and creating, "Cathay" joins "August Eschenburg"—as does "Snowmen"—in foregrounding the creative impulse as potentially manic, an obsessive effort to push back the limits of what art can represent. And "Cathay" even begins with bird automatons, fashioned from gold for the Emperor, not just to celebrate his august position but to prevent viewers from mistaking them for real birds.

In the interest of brevity, two examples of Cathay's obsession with miniatures must suffice. Miniaturists paint the eyelids of Court ladies with elaborate scenes so the women can expose them to courtiers they are interested in. They also paint landscapes on the areolae of the women's breasts, sometimes on the nipples too. More tellingly, a section entitled "Miniatures" describes a replica of the immense palace—so immense that when the Emperor investigated a wing he had never entered he was unsettled by finding descendants of his great-grandfather who spoke a different dialect. This replica, however, is small enough to sit on a table near the golden birds, yet it contains everything of the palace, including scissors small enough to hide behind a fly's leg. Legend has it that this replica in turn contains a replica so tiny that we might speculate the scissors could hide behind a molecule. In their compulsion to push against the limits of their arts, these miniaturists recall August with his irresistible but probably futile pursuit of the technology to achieve a perfect representation of human movement.

Here two major elements of Millhauser's fiction—the miniature and the replica—are melded. The Emperor's setting his craftsmen to work producing a miniature replica of his palace, with another miniature replica inside, demonstrates the author's pushing the concepts of replication and miniaturization beyond their limits and into fantasy. In his 1983 *Grand Street* essay, "The Fascination of the Miniature," the author argues that, unlike the gigantic which appalls us, the miniature draws us in, as "we yield to the miniature in sensual self-surrender" (130). At the same time, the miniature allows the viewer to possess it: a house is too large to take in at once, but a dollhouse can be so viewed. The miniature of the palace is also a replica, as Millhauser describes it in his 1995 *Yale Review* essay, a "haunted object" because in mimicking an original the replica emanates its dependence on an absent, and probably more perfect object, which the replica aspires to represent without a single flaw to erase its whole function.

The last, and only, section of "Cathay" to qualify as narrative is "The Contest of Magicians," whose winner will become the Court illusionist. The runner-up mystifies the Court by transforming a jade statue into a woman, perhaps the very model who had posed for the sculptor. When the winner also calls for a jade statue, the Court expects no more than a disappointing repetition of the earlier transformation. The Emperor declares this magician the winner, however, because his creation was neither an immobile statue nor a living woman but a moving statue that could breathe, a reminder perhaps of the artistic goal to create art that is *not* life but the illusion of life.

As a first collection of shorter fiction, *In the Penny Arcade* offers readers the broad spectrum of Steven Millhauser's interests. The three stories of Part II demonstrate his early attraction to the realist mode to which he never totally said farewell, returning to it often in the service of fantasy. "August Eschenburg" reveals his interest in what might be too quickly identified as "historical fiction," but which he finds useful in important stories, novellas, and novels, such as "Eisenheim the Illusionist," "The Little Kingdom of J. Franklin Payne," and his Pulitzer Prize novel, *Martin Dressler.* The first two stories in Parts II and III indicate his investment in narratives of childhood and the transition of adolescents into adulthood, foregrounded in his first two novels, *Edwin Mullhouse* and *Portrait of a Romantic.* In one sense "August Eschenburg" and "Snowmen" offer two masterpieces of what can be identified as Millhauser's distinctive style: a brilliant development of a realist narrative, replete with the scrupulous attention to detail that encourages readers to suspend disbelief that they are confronting "mere" fiction, and then moves them into a fantasy world in which we are so excited by the narrative's inventiveness that the extremes of imaginative production seem more real than the semblance of actuality out of which they were generated.

CHAPTER 6

The Barnum Museum

Like *In the Penny Arcade, The Barnum Museum* (1990) brings together fiction of varying lengths and raises the issue of form. Although length is obviously no reliable gauge of a story's significance, the longer stories in *The Barnum Museum* are likely to impress readers the most. The collection begins, for example, with a novella-length story, "A Game of Clue." The title story, "The Barnum Museum," may have fewer pages than a novella but has the feel of one. And "Eisenheim the Illusionist" has the impact of a novella without that form's customary length. Then too, this last story could become the best known because of Neil Burger's film adaptation, *The Illusionist* (2006). The Pulitzer Prize for *Martin Dressler, The Illusionist* film, and preliminary work on a film adaptation of "The Sisterhood of Night"[1] are bringing Millhauser's fiction to the attention of a larger audience.

Like "August Eschenburg," which opened the earlier collection, "A Game of Clue" establishes a realist, historical setting for its unexpected flight into fantasy.[2] Assuming readers lack experience with the board-game "Clue," the narrative describes the "Clue" board simply and completely, before the attentive reader is startled by an unexpected detail: one corner is covered by a saucer containing a burning cigarette. Thus the reality of the board-game is enclosed within the reality of the table on which it lies and the four players of "Clue," to be introduced. First, however, the narrator describes what else rests on the table in meticulous detail, including, for example, the label on the almost empty, red-wine bottle and the winery's lettering on a near-empty, souvenir wineglass. This is "realism" with a vengeance.

Once the narrative has offered an exhaustive description of the tabletop, down to a "scattering of brown crumbs," clearly bespeaking the realist mode, it goes on to the exquisitely scrupulous rendering of the mise-en-scène. This film term is not gratuitous, since the narrative recalls a film script, offering a set designer ample details to construct the scene. The narrative introduces a player—Jacob first—a struggling young poet, whose first section ends with his "solution" of the "whodunit": Colonel Mustard, with a revolver in the library. Then as though Jacob's imagination has projected the character, Mustard enters the library, without the revolver, and encounters Miss Scarlet.

This pattern is repeated again and again until all the characters/"players" in the "real world," all the "Clue" characters/"suspects," all the potential murder weapons and crime scenes are introduced. Then the narrative continues with these two plot-lines. One involves the dynamics of the relationships between the twenty-five-year-old Jacob, his twenty-four-year-old sister Marian, their fifteen-year-old brother David, whose birthday has occasioned the gathering, and Susan, Jacob's girlfriend, whom he insisted on bringing, without warning his family. This plot-line is "primary" because closer to our world, and yet the world of the six Clue suspects becomes equally compelling. They may be even *more* compelling, due to Millhauser's masterstroke in encouraging us to believe that the fantasy lives he has created for these inner-narrative, board-game emblems are more "real" than the lives of the fictional characters in the outer narrative.

Readers may be surprised to discover how successfully the narrative draws them into believing in these board-game "emblems." The narrative employs a Bakhtinian "de-familiarization" by voiding emblems of a numbing familiarity and empowering readers to see them through innocent eyes—a child's vision of the imagined inner being of ordinary objects, reminiscent of "Penny Arcade." The focus is not, for example, Professor Plum, exploring the secret passageways below, or Mrs. Peacock, wandering aimlessly, but Colonel Mustard and Miss Scarlet, and their bizarre relationship. Perhaps "sado-masochistic" is more appropriate to each vying for the power to humiliate the other—Colonel Mustard by forcing himself on Miss Scarlet sexually, while she submits to his possession to demonstrate the meaningless banality of his sexual assault. In this pastiche of What the Butler Saw,[3] or a contrived, voyeuristic vignette of rape in a sophisticated milieu, the two "characters" perform what turns out to be mere fantasy, not a "real" sexual encounter. Back of this narrative "performance," the narrator seems to be smirking and asking readers: Well, what did you expect of markers in a board game—a real encounter? How many sexual encounters are *not* merely the performances of sexual fantasies anyway?

Readers are more likely to be unsettled by uncertainty concerning the inner lives and the relationships of the "real" characters. Because "Clue" is a board-game variety of "Whodunit," readers look for "clues" to understand the foursome of players. The narrative strategy of moving from one brief segment to another, each with a title, draws readers into expecting less from, say, "Tokens and weapons" and more from "Marian," given her underdeveloped motivation. Readers learn she is fearful of ending up alone, or what's worse, in a "safe marriage" (*The Barnum Museum* 13–14). Her underdeveloped character results from her position in the family dynamic.

Jacob, Marian, and David Ross are an unusual trio of siblings. Because Jacob and Marian were ten and nine, respectively, when David was born—perhaps a happy accident after the parents thought their family was complete—he came to consciousness when his siblings were young adults. The parents are no more than fifty-somethings but as extraneous to the family as they are to the story. Readers encounter a surprising passage expressing David's profound love for his older brother, and eventually we learn that, after David spent his first three weeks in their parents' bedroom, he was moved into Jacob's room. Rather than resenting the intrusion, Jacob tenderly welcomed his baby brother. Because the infant strongly resembled his ten-year-old brother, Jacob felt as though *he* had "fathered" David. And Marian becomes her baby brother's surrogate-mother, who has continued to feel partnered with Jacob as David's mother. Thus her resentment toward Susan Newton, and perhaps any girlfriend Jacob brings home to meet the family, is understandable. Jacob's difficulty in maturing as a lover and as a poet, or more generally as a man, willing to move beyond an Edenic world of childhood's "Family Romance," as Sigmund Freud termed the relationship of child and parents, may be similarly understandable. Earlier, Jacob was so psychologically violent toward Susan that one of her passages is entitled "Jacob did it" (37), marking her perception of his murderous anger. Elsewhere Susan speculates that Jacob "wishes to confirm his sense of failure [as a poet] by failing with her" (21).

This "solution" to the puzzle of the Ross Family dynamic is based on the "clues" offered in the outside narrative. Readers are surprised by the David passages, expressing his intense love for Jacob and his preoccupation with women's breasts. One episode, however, is especially startling. As David recalls it, he casually entered his sister's bedroom, looking for a piece of paper or something else, and saw Marian's "heavy white breasts with their red wounds" (47). Readers expect clarification of how Marian's breasts were "wounded," but it never comes.[4]

Similarly, there are other anticipated clarifications and resolutions that readers are not offered. Is the relationship between Jacob and Susan promising, or is it what may be yet another dead end for a young man who has not grown away from a perhaps too-happy childhood? The lack of more complete development of Susan may be a "clue" to that relationship's eventual failure. Equally unresolved is the issue of whether Jacob has enough talent and drive to become a significant poet. And what of Marian, whose lack of development may not bode well for her transition into individual adulthood? The father's refusal to seek medical assistance after experiencing "shortness of breath" could serve as a metaphor for the siblings' difficulty in dealing with the actualities of the world outside the snug family nest.

By the story's ending, "A Game of Clue" has taken readers into the workshop of the storyteller and the craft of fiction. The "whodunit" framework of "Clue" reminds us of the detective story's low status and its irresistible attraction. Readers of "high art" may disdain the "whodunit" as "popular fiction" in spite of, or because of, its tremendous power to confirm the fugitive desire of readers to know at the end everything they did not know at the beginning. Shabby as the form and its gratification may seem, its power inheres in the wish that our lives could eventually promise the resolution and clarification represented by the answers to questions such as, who committed the crime and where/how was it done?

After the complexities and enigmas of "A Game of Clue," the next story, "Behind the Blue Curtain," *seems* a refreshing return to a more conventional narrative format. The unnamed boy narrator is dropped off at an American movie house, back in the 1950s. The situation recalls "In the Penny Arcade" in which a boy of twelve or thirteen also enters another dark world alone. Like the boy in "Penny Arcade," this narrator has an encounter with "another world," more explicitly sexual. Here it is what a young boy with a vivid imagination might expect to find not only on the other side of the movie theater curtain but behind the screen itself.

This boy has a college-professor father who has explained how film works.[5] The boy has played with old-fashioned "flip books," based on the notion of "persistence of vision," or the observation that the human eye can process only a certain number of images per second and when the maximum is exceeded the eye perceives them merging as continuous motion. The boy wants to believe in this magic of film—"My father was never wrong," he generalizes—"but I felt he was trying to shield me from darker knowledge" (61). It is that "darker knowledge" he is bent on exploring on this visit to the movies.

What he finds "behind the blue curtain" and the "silver screen" is a projection of a boy's fantasy of "real" performers, not the flat representation of single images on the screen. These performers, "backstage," are "splendidly costumed, radiantly themselves, expressing their natures through grand and flawless gestures" (65–66), while he is their audience of one, inspiring them "to be more grandly themselves" (67). They are delighted by his presence because "weren't they secretly in need of being watched, these lofty creatures, did they not become themselves through the act of being witnessed?" (67). The narrative offers a rendition of the philosopher Berkeley's notion that an object exists by virtue of its being perceived.

The boy wanders from one room to another, observing companies of performers, waiting to "go on stage." Presumably until the movie theater announces their show times, these figures are being "warehoused." One actress is especially important as an index of the boy's having entered puberty, for he is clearly aroused by her body, after he recognizes that she is performing for him. Her fainting spell, for example, was "executed with such elegance that [he] felt certain she had intended it to be admired" (69). Even more telling is his quasi-orgasmic sense of "falling through her, plunging through her corset, her breasts, her bones, her blood. . . . [His] whole body tingled . . ." (69). Seeing his waiting father frowning at his watch, he rushes away, and his father's "stern surprise" seems so "wildly funny" that he forgets to look repentant. The suggestion here is that the boy has undergone some rite of passage allowing him to grasp his father's hand as a fellow man.

The title story, "The Barnum Museum," exemplifies an approach to fiction that Millhauser will find increasingly attractive. Like "The Dream of the Consortium" and "Paradise Park" in *The Knife Thrower,* it is an architectural structure that becomes the "main character," and human beings in contrast are of minimal interest. Because the museum's name—"Barnum"—is never explained, readers assume it is a gesture toward P(hineas) T(aylor) Barnum, the nineteenth-century American entertainment entrepreneur, and trickster.[6] Millhauser's Museum suggests a similar self-conscious comic impulse; indeed his stories often partake of fictional forms deeply ingrained in American culture such as the "tall tale," or what Mark Twain's Huck Finn would call "telling a stretcher."[7]

"Barnum Museum" is "told" by another of Millhauser's first-person-plural narrators, a "we" taking readers on a tour of the establishment. Everything about the story is immersed in ambivalence. Is this museum one building or a complex of buildings made to look like one? Is it a compendium of differing architectural styles or a monstrosity daring the sophisticated to laugh at it as a hodgepodge of pretensions to "Kulchur"? How much is Millhauser as the creator of this museum himself a "Barnum," spoofing the Barnum-esque strain in American culture, at the same time that he is drawing his readers into almost believing in his "Hall of Mermaids" or gauging the reader's impulse to believe in ever-more fantastic phenomena? As the narrator claims, "there is often an atmosphere of carnival, of adventure" (76). As *New*

York Times reviewer Michiko Kakutani notes, the museum has a "darker, more sinister aspect" in its subterranean levels, containing what the narrator calls "disturbing creatures dangerous to behold.[8]

This is certainly no "museum" in the traditional European sense of specimens in glass cases with hard-to-read identifications in an atmosphere of cold, dark, dusty rooms, which go on endlessly—and tediously. Here the exhibits are continuously changing to create illusions of the "new." Pathways visitors took when entering the museum's inner exhibits are likely to be blocked and others opened to resemble a maze, enhancing the museum's sense of complexity and vastness. Architectural strategies shaping experiences of the museum include air ducts to lift skirts, an effort to reduce the somberness associated with museum-ing and add a flavor of "coarseness" (85). Despite their doubts, visitors irresistibly return, aware that they could live without the museum, but their lives would be diminished: "And is it possible the secret of the museum lies precisely here, in its knowledge that we can never be satisfied?" (91).

The next story, "The Sepia Postcard," is more conventional. Its first-person narrator is not so much the focus as the *whole* story. City life is so stressful that the narrator impulsively packs a bag in early September and heads for the New England coast, where he finds a picture-postcard world, but without the warm, sunny weather to complete the picture. The village—Broome—survives on the tourist trade, because it is full of shops, and the bored, tense, frustrated narrator claims to examine every shop window. Since he describes in extensive detail Plumshaw's Rare Books where he shops, readers believe his claim. Obviously he is not one on whom the smallest detail is lost.

Inevitably he buys the title's "sepia postcard," which readers have anticipated. The rainy, cold weather keeps him inside the room he leaves mainly for meals in the hotel's dining room, reminiscent of the play and film *Separate Tables,* emphasizing the loneliness and isolation of those not part of a "couple." He and a young woman are the only "singles," and much as he fantasizes meeting and marrying her, readers do not expect it to happen. The postcard comes to life for him as a little world of a couple sitting on a rock in the sun. As he gazes at the couple, their feelings become clearer as he "reads into" the picture his relationship with Claudia, as the man's face in the picture becomes "taut with fury" and the woman's face appears "stricken with terror" (107). In a clearly symbolic gesture, the narrator furtively returns the postcard and buys a bag of jellybeans he offers to share with the other "single," who tells him she does not like jellybeans. Driving out of town, he anticipates a weather change to warm sunshine, once the town disappears from his rearview mirror. Has the visit taught him something to improve his life? Readers are left less confident of his prospects than the boy's future in leaving the penny arcade.

The title of "The Eighth Voyage of Sinbad" draws in readers familiar with the seven *known* "Voyages" to ponder what "Eighth Voyage" Millhauser has constructed. That anticipation continues to the very end, as the story prepares for this "mythical" eighth voyage through a tripartite approach to the Sinbad story. The first three paragraph-segments establish the pattern for the story, with the first set in Sinbad's garden, to which he has retired after his voyages, followed by the second, offering a historical background for and commentary on the Sinbad stories, and the third, Sinbad's first-person narrative of his voyages. Readers learn in the second section that great European writers such as Shakespeare, Dante, and Cervantes knew nothing of Sinbad's Voyages because *The Arabian Nights* was not translated until the early eighteenth century.

The expository second section offers the justification for the last section, comprising Sinbad's telling of his voyages. This section asserts the limitations and contingencies of readings, no two of which are alike. Accordingly there are potentially as many voyages as there are readers. Witness an eighth voyage created by a boy reading Sinbad's second voyage on a hot summer afternoon in southern Connecticut, perhaps Millhauser's Stratford. In the midst of a family picnic scene, the boy longs to preserve his immersion in Sinbad's episode in the serpents' cave—desiring "this moment to last forever" (139). This desire to be both inside and outside the illusion of fiction mysteriously generates the last section of Sinbad's telling of an eighth voyage. It is produced by the boy's balancing his own capture by both the illusion of the story's reality and the realness of the actual world, enhancing that illusion's power. The story is classic Millhauser in its poignant yet unsentimental rendition of childhood in twentieth-century America.

The next three stories continue the collection's working outside the conventional short story. "Klassik Komix #1" is an "adaptation" of T. S. Eliot's landmark modernist poem "The Love Song of J. Alfred Prufrock" to "graphic fiction," or comic books, circling back to Edwin Mullhouse's "masterpiece" on comics or forward to Franklin Payne's marvelous animations and the brilliant "Cat 'n' Mouse." Readers may ponder if this story is spoofing Eliot's satirical portrait of the ineffectual Prufrock, using comic books as a genre of the "popular culture" Eliot looked down his nose at from his commitment to "high art."

Like "Komix" and the Sinbad story, "Alice, Falling" is another story demonstrating the range of Millhauser's intertextual relationships with "classics" of one kind or another. Like the Sinbad story, "Alice, Falling" offers yet another expression of Millhauser's sensitive rendering of childhood, here not the American childhood of the boy imagining an eighth voyage of the romantic hero of the "Arabian Tales," but Charles Dodgson's famous fictional character. Millhauser is attracted to Alice in a state of suspension between her real world where she sleeps in her sister's lap and the world of adventures to come. The seemingly endless fall down the rabbit-hole shaft allows the narrative to offer in great detail the titles of books on shelves and objects in niches along the way. Of interest here also is Dodgson writing the Alice story and recalling how he "sent [his] heroine straight down a rabbit-hole . . . without the least idea of what was to happen next" (170), leading some readers to speculate that Dodgson keeps Alice falling while searching for her destination.

"Rain" offers another expression of Millhauser's affection for scrupulously establishing a "real world" for a character to move in and for a reader to relate to, before allowing the story to slip over into fantasy. "Mr. Porter"—his given name is never divulged—comes out of a movie theater in a downpour. Running to his car and later getting out of it, when it stalls in knee-high water, Mr. Porter is more concerned with the water ruining his brand-new shoes, and even his shirt. He is an insubstantial character, ripe for the dissolution he seems to long for, since he thinks: "Have I wasted my life?" The deluge absorbs his shoes and clothes, then his body as so much "waste" to be washed away when he dissolves into a puddle of colored water. Once again a story invites us to read into the process of its making: Mr. Porter, the person and the two-dimensional character, wishes to be "erased," as the Mouse erases himself in the later story.

The penultimate story, "The Invention of Robert Herendeen," recalls earlier boyhood lives in *Edwin Mullhouse* and *Portrait of a Romantic*. Robert is a "different" boy, obsessed with details but highly imaginative, the product of an earlier stage of American culture before socializing young children became a priority. In college Robert had a double major in English and philosophy, which he "chose because they bore no relation whatever to actual life" (186). He reels off a number of projects he started and failed to complete. In his junior year he undressed (and presumably had sex with) a girl, and "was forced to make certain adjustments in the imaginary women who haunted [his] mind" (186). After graduating he was offered a year to decide on graduate school, or find a job, or do "something, anything" (186).

Robert succeeds in starting but never finishing projects and generally doing nothing other than imagining a girl—Olivia—into existence, in a modern rendition of the Pygmalion myth. Olivia visits him at night, but since she has no actual, tangible being, there is no possibility of a physical relationship. She is in essence no more than a figment of his imagination. Then she appears with the rude, obnoxious, intrusive Orville, whom Robert's imagination has also generated. Eventually Orville alienates Olivia's affection, and the story ends when Robert's imagination cannot support her, and along with her house she collapses into nothingness. Robert experiences what we might call a negative epiphany: he fails to see that his imagination is robbing his life of substance, and at the end he cautions himself to "remain calm" so he "might be able to imagine what would happen next" (214). This is a difficult story in large part because Robert essentially remains outside the reader's sympathy for his plight.

"Eisenheim the Illusionist" joins "August Eschenburg" as one of Millhauser's finest stories. It too follows the development of an artist in Central Europe about a century ago. Like August, and many other Millhauser characters, Eduard Abramowitz, later Eisenheim, is essentially a social isolate, and relatively little is known of his early life. This scarcity of information only adds to the aura of mystery in which he is shrouded after his radical self-transformation into the performance artist, who became famous enough to be only a last name—like Houdini. His ethnicity contributes to his isolation, for the narrative emphasizes that he was born into a Bratislavan Jewish family, his father being a cabinetmaker. At forty Eisenheim courts Sophie Ritter, whose landowner-father is a "staunch supporter of Lueger's anti-Semitic Christian Social Party.[9] Although Sophie loves Eisenheim, she rejects him and a month later marries a grain merchant, suggesting that Sophie's father discovered Eisenheim was a Jew.

Like the young August who encounters the automaton-maker in the green tent, Eisenheim as a boy has a formative experience with a magician sitting under a tree. After the magician runs through his repertoire of "magic tricks," he makes the tree and then himself disappear. Tellingly this dramatic finale occurs in *one* version of the story, providing a historical authenticity to the encounter through its indeterminate number of renditions. The encounter becomes formative in exciting the young Eduard's passion for magic tricks, but more importantly the magician's disappearance grounds Eisenheim's quest for the finale he performs to escape from arrest at the end.

The more significant element in Eduard's encounter with the traveling illusionist is the narrator's commentary on its finale. Readers may accept magic tricks such as plucking a coin from the boy's ear, but a magician's making a tree and then himself vanish are quite another thing. As though speaking over his narrator's shoulder, Millhauser comments: "Stories, like conjuring tricks, are invented because history is inadequate to our dreams" (217). This assertion clearly opens out to define fiction, especially Millhauser's, as necessitated by the spirit's hunger for imaginative sustenance in the meager world of "history," or actuality. Millhauser is leaving his workshop door ajar so readers see a justification for the plethora of realist detail to prepare for imaginative flights from the "real" world's inadequacies. And only a dozen or so lines later, the narrator voices Millhauser's perception again: "But who can unravel the mystery of the passion that infects an entire life, bending it away from its former course in one irrevocable swerve?" (217). These assertions offer this story a depth and resonance, empowering Millhauser's fiction as a whole.

Like August and that other automaton-maker, Heinrich Graum, Eisenheim soars to fame as a master of his art. Here the historical/cultural milieu is especially important. The narrator comments on a flowering of illusionism a century ago, on the brink of modernity. There is mention of the great illusionist Jean Eugène Robert-Houdin, whose name was recycled by Houdini.[10] Eisenheim masters the secret of Robert-Houdin's Orange Tree and others in the public repertoire before developing his own signature illusions. When he no longer has any rivals to his supremacy as the "foremost magician of his day," he invents and then unmasks himself as Eisenheim. Soon, like Heinrich Graum, Eisenheim becomes "burnt out" and disappears for the year 1900. Some say he could not face the nullity of that date's double zeroes, or in German "null-null."

When he returns in 1901, the first year of the new century—to be purist about when decades, centuries, and millennia begin—he has become a master artist. These new illusions involve invoking spirits of the dead. One of them—"Fraulein Greta"—was Marie Vetsera, who mysteriously died along with the Austro-Hungarian Crown Prince Rudolf in his hunting lodge at Mayerling. Eventually Eisenheim creates the illusions of other spirits, particularly children such as Elis and Rosa, who walk about and answer questions from the audience. This new departure calls up criticism from other illusionists who accuse Eisenheim of corrupting the art with "spiritualism," séances, and so forth. At this point Chief of Police Walther Uhl, a dabbler in magic, attempts to arrest the illusionist for "subverting the Empire." In Uhl's book, Eisenheim is guilty of "the crossing of boundaries" between illusion and reality, art and life. It is a high crime because an empire is itself an illusion, a tract of Nature, circumscribed by an imaginary line.

Uhl and the police fail to arrest Eisenheim because he has transformed himself into a spirit. Millhauser's description of the failed arrest offers some of his strongest writing. When the police officers attempt to lay a hand on Eisenheim, he "looked at them with an expression of such melancholy that one policeman felt a shadow pass over his heart" (236). Eisenheim's "unseeing eyes were dark autumn nights when the wind picks up and branches creak. . . . bending the black flame of his gaze inward, locked in savage concentration, he began to unknit the threads of his being" (236). Some observe "a look of fearful exaltation. Others . . . [hear] a cry of icy desolation" (236), and he is gone, never to be seen again.

CHAPTER 7

Little Kingdoms

Little Kingdoms (1993) once again raises issues of form in Steven Millhauser's fiction. This first of two collections of novellas is a reminder that he has published twice as many novellas as novels and published many more stories than novels and novellas combined. Despite the customary misconception that a novella is simply a short story that gets away from the writer, Millhauser has made it clear that he sits down to deliberately write a novella, rather than a story, and it is the time which elapses in the narrative that makes it a novella.[1] As he indicates, the novella is a risky venture because journal or magazine editors set limits on the length of short fiction they publish. Thus the novella becomes a potentially purer form, written for the writing of it, rather than the likelihood of immediate publication.

"The Little Kingdom of J. Franklin Payne" offers a classic example of Millhauser's mastery of the novella form.[2] Unlike "August Eschenburg" or "Eisenheim the Illusionist," which it resembles in certain respects, "Franklin Payne" begins in media res before it turns back to the formative experience in Franklin's boyhood. Just as August's art of automatons was shaped by his encounter with the paper figure animated by the frightened bird inside, or Eisenheim's career as an illusionist was formed by his encounter with the magician who made himself disappear, Payne's art as an animator had its origins while he assisted his father in the darkroom. In later life, Payne recalls his father's voice as he slowly counted the seconds for the paper to remain in the enlarger, while moving his finger up and down, as though he were a priest celebrating the mystery of how the photographic image miraculously came into being, after being called to the darkroom like a spirit from the beyond.

The excitement the boy Franklin felt in the quiet reverence of the darkroom was recaptured when he put pencil or crayon to white paper, and images again seemed to generate themselves from nothing. After immersing himself as a college student in Klein's Wonder Palace—one of Millhauser's signature museums, comprising a movie theater, freak shows, and a collection of old wax figures—Franklin is offered a part-time job doing advertising posters and quick-sketch portraits. Eventually he is noticed by a newspaperman and offered a job in the Cincinnati *Daily Crier*'s art department. Soon he creates a comic strip, set in Klein's dime museum, and calls the strip "Dime Museum Dreams." As Franklin moves into jobs with greater responsibility and higher pay, the narrative becomes more clearly a bildungsroman, or story of an individual's development. Accordingly he becomes a forerunner of Martin Dressler, an "American dreamer," motivated by the excitement of self-transformation.

J. Franklin Payne confirms his success by marrying Cora Vaughn, daughter of a Cincinnati judge, and then moving his wife and their three-year-old daughter Stella to New Hebron, in upstate New York. Franklin divides his energies between his job as a staff artist at the *New York World Citizen,* where he does political cartoons as well as a comic strip, and his avocation as an animator. In the opening scene, having finished his "homework" on the comic strip, he turns to his labor of love, meticulously creating india-ink drawings on pieces of rice paper for an animated cartoon for which it will take 4,000 "pages" for a four-minute cartoon. He is working on page number 1,827.

The narrative strategy of extended flashback in the second chapter allows the story to proceed some days after Franklin's "enchanted night" of climbing out his window to celebrate the wonder of this starry night. To some, he will seem the child who refuses to "grow up," but to the author, one suspects, Franklin retains the penny-arcade boy's recuperated innocence, the capacity to *see* with a child's eyes, crucial to creativity. As becomes overt, Franklin's childlike innocence as an adult will recall August's, especially as Max Horn comes on stage to reprise the role of Hausenstein.

The timing of Horn's visit to Franklin's home is crucial, for everything follows from the entry of Horn.[3] Central to this first visit is Horn's surprise that Franklin never mentioned having a wife and Cora's "coolly" matching the visitor's remark to indicate *her* surprise that he had been invited. If Horn's remark implies that Franklin has "forgotten" he has a wife or was keeping her hidden from potential rivals, Cora cannot go so far as to say Franklin has been "hiding" Horn but does indicate surprise that her husband did not mention the invitation.

Readers are able to sense the "chemistry" between Cora and Horn because the second chapter's flashback has taken them back to the beginning of this strange marriage. Initially Cora resisted Franklin's overtures because she saw drawing comic strips as no respectable occupation. Additionally Cora is attached to her father, spending as much time in the judge's home as her husband's. More telling, however, is her persistent distancing of Franklin, insisting, for example, that he sleep in a separate bedroom. The Paynes were not unique in sleeping alone. Nevertheless, Franklin is put on notice that Cora will initiate lovemaking, traditionally a male function, and soon learns she will become angry if he "disturbs her sleep." It is probably not coincidental that Stella is born nine months after Cora surprised Franklin by seeking *him* out in his bedroom. This flashback is crucial to forestalling the misreading of her adultery as resulting from his neglect as he invests himself in animation.

The narrative registers Cora's unexpected behavior during Max's first visit through the innocent eyes of Franklin, whose great concern had been that Cora would have a "bad impression" of his friend. To the contrary, Cora seems more open and warm than usual, sharing with Max impressions and experiences from her past that she may not have ever revealed to Franklin. In Max's presence, Cora certainly is less self-restrained, letting the screen door slam behind her when she goes in for crackers and cheese, or bumping it with her hip in a gesture of "slight immodesty," which arouses a husband who hopes she will take him to bed. Instead, she encourages Franklin and Max to "stay up and talk" (*Little Kingdoms* 44), a surprising turn-off for her husband and a hint to readers that it may not be Franklin who has excited her impulse to get to bed.

What follows is emblematic of Franklin's arrangement of his erotic and creative lives. With Cora's having metaphorically slammed her bedroom door in his face, Franklin invites Max to his study, where his work seems in part a compensation for the deprivation of a healthy erotic life. Franklin shares with Max his secret project—the four-minute cartoon. Max is appalled by Franklin's "waste of time" in re-drawing each sheet completely, when he could reuse the background and merely make the minimal changes in subsequent sheets. Franklin's response to the pragmatic Max—reminiscent of August's reaction to Hausenstein's cynical disparaging of his artful automaton-making—is a sense of betrayal. His friend has failed to *see* this painstaking work as a labor of love. Max succeeds in changing the subject, and ends with the request that Franklin tell Stella he is "madly in love with her" (47), a request—as readers eventually see—Max probably hoped might be expressed within Cora's earshot.

Max's anticipated second visit produces differing anxieties for both Paynes. Franklin worries it will be a letdown after the first, or merely a lost opportunity to work on his animations, which are entering a critical stage. Cora is anxious that everything will be perfect, tellingly changing her *dress* twice and more to the point asking the housekeeper to clean the mirrors again, even though she has planned a picnic on a wooded hilltop, where Max has the entree to reveal his desire to buy land nearby and build a house. When they return and Franklin excuses himself for two minutes to continue the story he is telling Stella, he comes down from work in his study two hours later, guilty about having left Cora to entertain Max and grateful to his friend for "getting on so well with Cora" (48). By this point readers should have begun to suspect that the innocent husband is just not seeing what is going on here. Once again the background of the Paynes' courtship and marriage is crucial because it foregrounds the distinct possibility that Cora finally married Franklin because he was willing to live at a distance and accept her mere tolerance of his presence.

The aftermath of this second visit is Franklin's dramatic invitation that Max accompany him to an undisclosed site. Franklin surprises his friend, and readers, by taking Max to a screening of the four-minute-and-twelve-second *Dime Museum Days,* in which Franklin's meticulous crafting of each sheet has created marvelous perspective, impossible in the faster "cel" technique. Franklin is surprised by an outburst of applause from the projectionist and two studio employees, but even more by the excitement in Max's glittering eyes, perhaps momentarily recuperating the boy Max's innocent vision. This is a moment of triumph for Franklin, impelling him toward his next masterpiece, whose completion will cost him his marriage.

Along the way, the August-Hausenstein conflict in Franklin and Horn grows. Horn is flabbergasted that Franklin is so dissatisfied with *Dime Museum Days* that he replaces 2,000 of the 4,236 rice-paper drawings. Franklin is an "amateur," or lover, willing to lavish time to nurture its development, just as he provides Stella with quality time because Cora neglects her. When *Dime Museum Days* enjoys nationwide release, Max joins Franklin in the audience, but Cora is unsurprisingly absent. Franklin allows himself to gloat by later showing Max a review in which his film is lauded for its "scrupulous draftsmanship," setting it apart from inferior forms of animation and marking its movement into art (55).

The success of *Dime Museum Days* has its price. His boss Alfred Kroll accuses him of investing company time and energy in a personal project he sees as based on the newspaper's comic strip. That stress, along with the strain and long hours of completing the film, takes its toll on Franklin's health. Perhaps not coincidentally, Max proceeds with his purchase of land nearby and the construction of a home in the extended "neighborhood." The rest required to restore Franklin's health is fruitful, however, and he creates a new comic strip, "Adventures in Underland," about a boy's experience in subways and tunnels, which Kroll likes but renames "Subway Sammy." Franklin's "Underland" adds to Millhauser's earlier underworlds in *From the Realm of Morpheus* and "Alice, Falling."

The success of "Subway Sammy" ushers Franklin into his next major period of creativity. When Stella becomes ill again, and Cora does not conceal her impatience with their daughter, Franklin makes flip books to amuse his ill child. He imagines a new animation into being—*Toys at Midnight*—whose central figure is a doll, which comes to life in a world of increasingly fantastic adventures, an anticipation of the mannequin and dolls in *Enchanted Night.* As these animations focus on adventures of a doll created for Stella and in part a representation of Stella herself, Franklin's daughter becomes his assistant. As Cora fades from the scene, Stella and Franklin invest themselves more fully in what eventually becomes for both an alternative reality.

Cora's fading away from her *family,* not merely her husband, is unmistakable in the housewarming party Max throws. When father and daughter go rowing while waiting for Cora to return from shopping, Stella tells her father "sharply" that "Mom hates to go anywhere with us" (86). Waiting for them at home is Cora's note, indicating she has "run into" Max in town and gone to help set up the party at which Stella and Franklin are expected at 5:30. The narrator indicates: "It was half-past three" (86), suggesting that Franklin is finally confronting Cora's infidelity. At the party Max and Cora are clearly a couple, and he even jokingly introduces Franklin to Cora as his friend. Franklin later discovers Stella is nowhere to be seen, arousing the reader's anxiety that something has happened to her. When he finds her and she asks when they can go home, Franklin sits down and the next thing he knows Max is appropriately "awakening" them.

Because Max's studio—"Maxograms, Inc."—will be producing *Toys at Midnight,* Max becomes his "boss." Not surprisingly he is appalled by Franklin's wish to redo many drawings and demands that the revised project be completed in a month. Franklin meets the deadline in twenty-nine days, but the cost is immense. He returns from work to discover Cora's "I can no longer live a lie" note, and although he attempts to shelter Stella from the truth, eventually she ends the charade by telling him her mother will never return. Out of the pain of being betrayed by his wife and his best friend comes the germ of his next project. He already has chosen a title, *Voyage to the Dark Side of the Moon*—shades of Morpheus!—and knows it will be his longest animation, with a run-time of thirty minutes, requiring 30,000 drawings.

The project's scope would have been daunting to a young Franklin, even without his devastating discoveries. The artist appears to be flirting with tragedy, joining Millhauser's other tragic artists such as August, Eisenheim, and preeminently Martin Dressler to come. It is scarcely accidental that among Millhauser's most memorable creations are these tragic overreachers who are constitutionally unable to settle for less or to resist the modernist impulse to pursue ever-more unrealizable expressions of their creative imaginations.

For this perhaps last project, Stella more fully becomes Franklin's assistant and consultant. Because they work together at night, the story's world is appropriately done in black-and-white.[4] Color *is* entering animations, and there have been experiments with sound. Franklin, however, sees the essence of animation in a winter night: "the world was silent and black-and-white" (104). Like August Eschenburg, Franklin is clearly moving toward the end of his art, an art that will soon be a historic artifact, or more negatively an "antique."

Increasingly Franklin becomes more theoretical about his art's essentially black-and-white nature. Paradoxically the motion picture creates the illusion of motion, light, and life from stasis, darkness, death, through the often-noted "persistence of vision," based on the retina's limited capacity to process individual images and the eventual merging of an image with its immediate predecessor. If anything, film animation is more "honest" than realist film because it foregrounds its illusion-making as the successful accomplishment of the impossible. Indeed, to quote Franklin's reflection, "The animated cartoon was nothing but the poetry of the impossible," providing both the "exhilaration" of violating the actual as well as the "melancholy," or the deathliness of its delusion that the impossible can be achieved.

Drawn deeper into that "poetry of the impossible," Franklin further savors the metaphoricity of his materials. He continues to draw in black ink on white rice paper, but he will ask the photographer of the drawings of the "dark side of the moon" to print the negative so that the figures are white against a black background, allowing his hero to undergo fantastic metamorphoses in the dead world. And when the film is completed and ready to screen in his study for Stella's eyes, Franklin pushes the metaphor of light and darkness even further, troping the projector's beam as the modern world's "moonbeam," casting its light and its illusion of life on the white movie screen.

Although there are two novellas to follow, so that readers cannot depend on the number of subsequent pages to signal the story's ending, they have the sense of an ending here. In the first reel's screening, Cora appears to join the audience, followed by Max. During the second reel, the narrative strains credibility by the appearance of Kroll, the enemy of his two earlier animations. But it *is* still within the range of possibility. The appearance of Franklin's dead parents during the third, and final, reel, however, discloses how Millhauser's narrative is now clearly mirroring its own content by foregrounding itself as the "poetry of the impossible." Obviously the parents are dead. In this reel of the moon's dark side, the hero in white wields a chalkboard eraser, gradually erasing himself and leaving behind only the eraser of his life in the dark, lifeless world of his self-extinction—a strategy replicated in the short story "Cat 'n' Mouse" in *Dangerous Laughter.* As the scene performs itself, Franklin, who is hallucinating the presence of his parents, has made the final move, joined perhaps by Stella, into an alternative world whose satisfactions transcend our "real," and therefore ultimately unsatisfying world. The powerful ending combines the tragedy of recognition that our world may have no room for the Franklins and Stellas with the "comedy" of witnessing Millhauser's brilliant delineation of art's transcendent capacity to express the "poetry of the impossible."

"The Princess, the Dwarf, and the Dungeon" represents Millhauser's continuing attraction to fantasy, or more specifically, the fairy tale. It begins with a young Prince who marries a Princess, as beautiful as he is handsome. For a year they live happily, until he persuades himself his wife and a visiting margrave are lovers. When the Prince (he and the Princess are unnamed) approaches the Princess and margrave alone together in a "small receiving chamber attached to her private rooms" (122), her response to her husband's sudden appearance is tantalizingly ambiguous. Jolted out of her "revery," she impulsively puts her hand to her throat, and is both "startled" and "flushed." Later the narrator will reveal what the Prince never knows: The margrave has told the Princess that his wife was kidnapped and murdered. Indeed her "revery" may have been produced by empathy for his suffering. The Prince may laugh off his suspicions, but the spawn of his later monstrous jealousy has been conceived.

The narrative focuses upon the Prince's increasingly perverse cultivation of his jealousy. When he and the Princess walk in their orchard, he picks a pear to give her, but she offers to cut the pear in half to share, imploring him to reveal what is bothering him. Because he is ashamed that he has doubted her fidelity, the Prince discloses only his fear of the margrave's "dishonest intentions toward him" (127). In ardently defending the margrave's integrity, the Princess further arouses the Prince's jealousy, as does Desdemona by advocating the case of Cassio, who Iago has intimated to Othello is his cuckolder. Millhauser's Prince is his own Iago, proposing that she test their sleeping guest's improper desires. His immodest proposal and her horrified consent are nicely imaged by the pear's slipping from her hand and falling to the ground, where its "split skin" is exposed. Seeing in his wife's face the terror of "someone frightened in the dark" has now "made the prince taste the full horror of his moral fall, even as it sharpened the sting of his suspicions" (127). It is no coincidence that the Prince has become the lower-case "prince."

The prince is "soothed" by his wife's report that the margrave passed the "honor" test, but the actual presence of his wife in another man's bed has further unsettled the prince. Jealousy feeds upon itself, as the prince insists on further "proof" because the margrave may have simply not been prepared to enjoy his host's wife. Although the Princess swears that "she would sooner plunge a dagger into her heart" (131), her husband eventually drives her back to the field of honor. No number of passed tests can persuade the prince who perversely *needs* the evidence of adultery to give him peace by removing the uncertainty. Besides, how can innocence be *proved*?

Then the narrative introduces the only named character—Scarbo, the dwarf—a figure reminiscent of Scurlock in *From the Realm of Morpheus*. Supernaturally infused with evil impulses, Scarbo is also the most complex of the four characters. He possesses a sensitivity conventionally considered "feminine." Like women, the dwarf is an outsider in a patriarchal world that forces the powerless to learn how to accommodate themselves to the needs and desires of powerful men. To Scarbo, the prince's Achilles' heel is a "desire for immense suffering" (138), a desire that not even the prince recognizes. Essentially Scarbo is the prince's avatar, an older, "deformed" version of his master.

As the servant of his master's unholy desires, Scarbo is ordered to keep the Princess under twenty-four-hour surveillance. He relishes skulking in the margrave's bed chamber, listening for the sounds of adultery as the "ears" of a master too embarrassed to do what he sends his henchman to do. Scarbo is shrewd enough to foresee the dire consequences of bearing witness against the Princess, lest the prince "shoot the messenger." And the dwarf seems genuinely surprised to hear only the sounds of silence, leading him to find his "brilliantly simple" strategy and to make his own immodest proposal. He proposes that the Princess should denounce the margrave and thereby fulfill the prince's need to suffer. The Princess is appalled by the dwarf's proposal, especially after the margrave has told of his wife's brutal murder. Eventually her health is destroyed in her resisting Scarbo's proposal and his twisted logic that the margrave must desire her, and even friendship is a passion. Looking into the darkness of her heart, the Princess is persuaded that the margrave is guilty and she denounces him to the prince, who immediately throws him in the dungeon to be tortured and condemns his wife to the psychological torture of knowing she is an accessory to that torture.

Next the plot takes another unexpected turn, when the Princess summons Scarbo to her room. Well aware her "treason" places her in the dwarf's absolute power, she entreats him to ameliorate the margrave's horrible circumstances and help him escape. In the long section "Dwarf in the Tower," describing in detail Scarbo's work in helping the margrave, while anticipating the pleasure the Princess will give him, the narrative changes dramatically to emphasize the concerns of the prince's subjects that an escaped margrave might go home to muster a great army and invade the princedom to revenge himself for being tortured almost to death.

Immediately following this "Invasion" section, in which the voice of the community foregrounds itself as a Millhauserian first-person-plural narrative, the novella produces the long-awaited section "A Disturbing Episode" of Scarbo's movement toward gratifying his lust. Readers should note that Millhauser signals the dwarf's total immersion in rape fantasies in a six-page paragraph. Approaching her bedchamber, with a dagger to force her compliance, Scarbo screens erotic images of the Princess submitting to his lust. His desire begins to cool, however, when he must endure her icy disdain as he stretches to grasp the doorknob, can barely look over the bed's edge, and must climb three steps to walk across to her. As his lust wilts, the dwarf tenders the dagger to the Princess to defend herself "against unwelcome guests" (165) and transforms the Princess into a saint of love, who overwhelms him with her strength of character and courage in engineering the margrave's release.

The voice of the community dominates the remaining narrative, emphasizing its being based on legends. This communal narration affects the story's ending(s), denying readers an ending but cataloging instead the potential endings. Choosing a single ending is to be satisfied with a "bare and diminished thing, like a tree with a single branch" (170) and denying potential endings and their "secret kinship" with each other. These possible endings are all "instances of a single ending, in which injustice resolves in justice, and discord in concord" (170). These endings credit hope, without resorting to an ending that imposes a limited "meaning" on the story.

With its long title, "Catalogue of the Exhibition: The Art of Edmund Moorash (1810–1846)," this third novella announces the exhibition of a fictional early nineteenth-century artist's work. The birth-and-death dates indicate a "retrospective." Lacking reproductions of the works it describes, the catalog compels readers to imagine them from often meager descriptions, particularly as the narrative overpowers the catalog device. Since each entry emphasizes Moorash's life, especially his "difficult" personality, the paintings serve more as texts to read the artist than as expressions of any particular artistic merit. Like Jeffrey Cartwright, the catalog-writer finds the biographical approach to art irresistible.

The catalog-narrative stratagem has a major asset in facilitating the economical rendering of the lives of Moorash, his family, and friends. "Moorash" can be immensely more selective in providing the story of approximately two decades of the artist's life. The challenge, however, is the flip side of that exhibition-catalog approach of delegating what amounts to the entire narrative responsibility to an anonymous, impersonal catalog-writer. Such an approach lays significant demands on readers to "read between the lines," at the risk of "reading into" the text.

The location and even the dating of the exhibition are left open, omissions justified by the reader's supposedly holding the catalog in hand. Since one painting was not discovered until 1951, the exhibition and its catalog presumably date from the later twentieth century. And we can deduce that the catalog-writer is an art historian. Here is nothing like the elaborate, brilliantly entertaining framework for *Edwin Mullhouse,* comprising the introduction to Jeffrey's "biography" by an academic who happened upon the book whose author he claims to have met when they were briefly elementary-school classmates.

The early entries provide a brief introduction to the young-adult Moorash. No child prodigy, the painter began drawing at Harvard in the late 1820s. Moorash was an eccentric; he painted fellow-student William Pinney's portrait, for example, but refused to paint portraits for money, choosing to paint panels for fire trucks instead. Additionally the catalog-writer introduces Moorash's sister Elizabeth through her portrait, deemed by the cataloger "Moorash's early masterpiece" (184), even though it was ridiculed by critics.

Perhaps it was these bad reviews that turned Moorash against the art world. In the entry for "The Infernal Picture Academy," the catalog-writer describes a picture in which Moorash the satirist includes several copyists at work in the gallery to add the playful confusion of the "real" paintings and their painted copies. This painting was to be one of eight commissioned by an art collector. Moorash failed to fulfill the commission because in his estimation galleries are "those most fashionable of graveyards with their numbered headstones" (186). Elsewhere he called paintings in a gallery "a line of prisoners waiting to be shot" and spoke of the "necessary evil" of art galleries (187). The "grotesque" and "sadistic" aspects link the painting to a fictional "Diabolist movement" (189), anticipating Moorash's growing attraction to the demonic.

Later entries increasingly introduce paintings merely to "move the story forward." The paintings' subjects become a dramatis personae of what later purports to be a tragic tale of unruly emotions and conflicts of love interests. The "Figures in the Snow" of #9, threatened by a menacing snowstorm, may be Elizabeth and Moorash's college friend William Pinney, who loves her. In

"Elizabeth at Dusk: Black Lake," Elizabeth is an "unrecognizable figure," merely "inspirational" to Moorash. The catalog-writer seems to be "reading into" their vague representations to find ample grist for his/her storytelling. The likelihood of Moorash's blocking Elizabeth's marriage is implied in his casting her for the next painting as "Thorn Rose," the beautiful girl surrounded by a wall of thorns, a figure that occurred memorably in *Edwin Mullhouse.*[5]

The calamitous ending of the "story" is foreshadowed by the "coincidence" of death dates. Elizabeth's journal notes the visit of the "girlish wife, Charlotte (1823–1846)" of the "older Vail." In the next entry the sister of Elizabeth's love-interest William is introduced as "Sophia Pinney (1816–1846)." Readers may find themselves refreshing their memories of Moorash's dates—1810–1846—and William Pinney's—1808–1846. With increased heartbeats, Sherlockholmesing readers look for Elizabeth's death date, 1846. Some may begin to Google "1846" for details of a calamity that year in the Northeast, as the narrative is shaping up to become a thriller: How are all these people going to die in one year?

A calamity *will* strike the characters, but it is of their own making. In entry #13, "Clair de Lune," when William Pinney proposes marriage to Elizabeth, Moorash is "shocked" since he felt "virtually married to" Elizabeth. Four days later, "for the sake of Edmund's art," she rejects the proposal. Sometime earlier, Moorash had playfully said that, if his sister were not around, his "absentmindedness" might cause him to starve to death. The sophisticated cataloger may caution readers not to misunderstand the brother-sister relationship as "banal perversion" and add it was not certain Elizabeth actually loved Pinney. Moorash, however, apparently never encouraged his sister to accept his friend's proposal.

Thus far, the distance and the impersonal tenor of the cataloger-narrator's entries pose few problems. Readers are drawn forward through these ersatz catalog-entries toward finding out what killed off the dramatis personae. That question will lead to yet others: What is the mode of this novella? What relationship to the portended calamity is the cataloger-narrator modeling for readers? The narrative appears to be moving toward a "tragedy" involving the deaths of five people within a year, while continuing to maintain the masquerade of describing paintings by a minor "artist." Has Millhauser delegated the storytelling function to a reliable narrator? Or, is there another narrator-figure backstage, so to speak, cuing readers to look beyond the cataloger's responses to this tragedy, to something closer to farce? Clearly Millhauser has done something similar in encouraging readers to see Jeffrey's "biography" as confessional fiction, whose narrator is a murderer.

This issue of narrative-mode surfaces more blatantly in the next entry, "Nachtstück," or "Night Piece." Married to a man almost old enough to be her grandfather, Charlotte Vail falls victim to a "wasting disease" and confesses her passionate love—surprisingly enough, for Moorash. Readers are even less prepared, however, for the immodest proposal Charlotte's husband makes in entreating Moorash to come immediately to "save" Charlotte. When Charlotte was introduced the year before in the story, the cataloger indicated she was sixteen "but looked two years younger" (197), suggesting that Moorash is a son of Poe in his attraction to Vail's child-bride. After Moorash spends the night at Rose Cottage, Charlotte's health improves, but a total recovery will require Moorash to visit her three times a week.

Because the cataloger appears completely responsible for the narrative, readers may have difficulty deciding what the tone is here. The cataloger-narrator seems incredibly naive to believe readers will accept Moorash as a medical miracle-worker whose "patient" can recover only if he spends every other night with her. In his "innocence," or pretense of it, the cataloger is apparently unaware of the ironic title "Night Piece" for Moorash's painting. Readers, however, may smile at the implication that it was not his muse Elizabeth who inspired the painting; it was the "night piece" he enjoyed while valiantly attempting to save poor Charlotte from an unusually early death. In his naïveté this cataloger seems related to the fictional Professor White, who was totally unaware that Jeffrey's "biography" of Edwin was an oblique confession to murder. Indeed there are subtle suggestions of connections with Millhauser's first novel, whose title character had the same initials, "E.M." and "Edmund" might be easily confused with "Edwin."

Foreshadowing the ending, it is Elizabeth, not Edmund Moorash, who becomes central to the inevitable calamity. Moorash literally cannot live without Elizabeth, and Sophia blames Moorash for standing in the way of her brother's happiness. What's more, Sophia appears to care for Elizabeth as more than a friend, significant as a rare occurrence of a same-sex relationship in Millhauser's fiction. The bizarre story has another twist in store for readers when Moorash declares his love for Sophia, perhaps as a surrogate for Elizabeth, whom he cannot love "romantically." Now readers see why the cataloger developed Moorash's therapeutic romance with Charlotte, for they may not have noticed the total absence of any romance for Moorash, much less sexuality, until at thirty he "saved" Charlotte.

From this point, readers struggle to follow the labyrinthine course of the foursome's feelings. Moorash's painting at the time is *Totentanz,* or "Dance of Death," foreshadowing the story's approaching climax. After Moorash tells her, "All paintings are ghosts" (218), Elizabeth reads the foursome in the painting's dancers. Moorash *may* be saying that, once the artist finishes the work, the painting exists only as a ghostly specter of the creative process that produced it, but he also may be pre-viewing the coming disaster.

Amidst all this fine talk of Art, the cataloger is offering a foursome embroiled in a melodrama[6] of lovers and friends acting at cross purposes, reminiscent of the occasional playful staging of *Hamlet* as farce. This long "Totentanz" entry is lengthened by Moorash's recuperated pursuit of Sophia, who disdains him. Then too, Elizabeth is jealous and resentful of her brother's "betrayal" of her love for him when she relinquished Pinney to save her brother. Sophia resents Elizabeth's blaming her for rejecting Moorash's love, with its possibility of a marriage producing a *ménage à trois*. And Pinney is peeved not only by the lingering presence of his "friend" Moorash as an impediment to marrying Elizabeth, but also Moorash's pursuit of Pinney's sister, suggesting a desire to capture "all the women" (220). Readers may wonder if Pinney knows about Moorash's "medical miracle" in saving Charlotte Vail. Were it not for the looming death dates, readers might imagine a happy ending in which the foursome might marry and retire to a super king-sized bed to work out their thwarted desires, with Charlotte occasionally joining them when she feels a recurrence of her "wasting disease" with a spouse on whom her youth is apparently "wasted."

Instead, the cataloger chooses to see this romantic tale as "tragedy." Once again Elizabeth plays the central role. Sophia "passionately" believes that Moorash's lethal hold on his sister is not only blocking Elizabeth's marriage to William but destroying her health and robbing Sophia of her true love. Sophia is also shocked by Elizabeth's proposing to marry Pinney if Sophia will marry Moorash. Sophia almost agrees, despite her suspicion its "secret cause" is Elizabeth's perhaps final service to her brother's needs and therefore a denial of love for Sophia, much less Pinney. Then Elizabeth withdraws her proposal, essentially condemning herself and the others to death.

In the long final entry, *SELF-PORTRAIT,* the cataloger's ending will remind some of the corpse-strewn stage in Act V of *Hamlet.* Just after Elizabeth dies, the Pinneys arrive. Overcome with grief and rage at Moorash's having "killed" her friend, Sophia slashes the self-portrait with sewing scissors, before plunging them into her own throat. Belatedly Moorash pulls the scissors from Sophia's throat and in wrestling for control of them with Pinney, the artist is fatally wounded. When the housekeeper enters the room, she discovers Pinney dead with an arm stretched toward Elizabeth's corpse. Pinney also died of a stab wound, presumably from the sewing scissors. That the deadly weapon which slew all four figures was a pair of *sewing scissors* does little to elevate this story to "tragedy."

Furthermore, the cataloger's interruption of the ending to comment on unsuccessful attempts to restore the slashed self-portrait crowns the comedy here. Its coup de grâce is the last sentence, reporting the death some months later of Charlotte Vail, "after a lingering death" to which she was presumably condemned with the passing of her "medicine man," who had only *seemed* to cure her "wasting disease." Tragedy demands access to the subject's interiority, allowing its audience to care about the subject's death. Lacking such access, "tragedy" becomes mere pathos, or at its extreme, farce.

Together, these three novellas explore the themes of betrayal and jealousy, evident again in the next trio of novellas in *The King in the Tree* (2003). *Little Kingdoms* demonstrates the spectrum of Millhauser's investments in the past—early twentieth-century America, medieval Europe, then early nineteenth-century America. If it is the "sense of an ending"[7] that points toward meaning, readers may find a range in these novellas from tragedy in "Franklin Payne" to pathos or comedy in "Princess," where the ending offers hope that all will be well, and finally tragedy, replayed as farce in "Moorash."

CHAPTER 8

Martin Dressler

Steven Millhauser's Pulitzer Prize–winning novel, *Martin Dressler* (1996), will remind readers of his earlier novels such as *Edwin Mullhouse* and shorter fiction such as "August Eschenburg" and "Eisenheim the Illusionist." *Martin Dressler* is a bildungsroman, following the development of yet another self-immersed dreamer/artist who lives for the pursuit of his own ideals and goals, with a minimal concern for financial success or relationships with others.

The ambivalence of the novel's subtitle—*The Tale of an American Dreamer*—aptly catches the story's double nature. It is a story of that quintessential American Dream, the concept of personal self-development—both spiritual to the idealist and economic to the pragmatist. But it is also the "tale" of a "dreamer," with its own ambivalence—one who aspires and one who is no longer in touch with actuality. Martin at eight is a "dreamer" of a larger world beyond the narrow confines of his father's tobacco shop and the cramped living quarters above, especially his small room.

The setting over a century ago locates the narrative in a more innocent time in the United States—or so the myth proclaims—to embody in Martin the "American Dream" in its earlier and purer form. Dressler is no John D. Rockefeller, aspiring to immense wealth and power, but the representative of the Old Country's dream of a New World in which to dream oneself into a larger, more complex and more splendid state of being.[1] Any success Martin achieves only whets his appetite for greater dreams of the ultimate "hotel" as a world within the world. Because Dressler, like Eschenburg or Eisenheim, pushes himself to ever-greater achievements, this novel's mode is essentially tragic. As Dressler himself senses, to rest upon his laurels as a visionary of the ultimate hotel is to accept a more ignominious defeat than to dream up worlds that are ever-more impractical for those he expects to move into these "castles in the air." To dream the impossible and not achieve it may be tragic, but such "failure" certifies the value of the dream, while being satisfied with actuality is to deny the grandeur of American dreaming of self-transformation.

As in his other renditions of personal development, Millhauser focuses on those aspects of Martin's childhood that foreshadow the central issues of his adult life. The opening sentence draws readers into the story as a "tale" to be *told,* a fable—"There once lived a man . . . who rose from modest beginnings to a height of dreamlike good fortune" (*Martin Dressler* 1). The "American Dream" of self-transformation as a nineteenth-century construct is underlined by its being a *romantic* dream of satisfying the "heart's desire" (2), rather than a tawdry effort to "get rich quick." Even as a boy, Martin dreams of a life and a world that his parents could scarcely imagine.

Accordingly Martin's parents, especially his father, represent crucial formative elements. Otto Dressler came to America seeking the Promised Land, but like Moses he gets no more than a Pisgah view because he is too timid, too beaten down by the Old Country to do more than beget a son who will dream the Dream. Central to Martin's early development is his construction of the cigar-tree for his father's shop-window. Martin gets the idea for this display while on a customary Sunday stroll with his mother past shop-windows, dazzling him with the rich plenitude of the great world beyond his father's little shop. Otto Dressler allows Martin to construct the tree, even though in his little world of self-denial the cigar-tree is potentially "extravagant." Because his father is an inhibiting force, Martin ends in disappointment and frustration after having to scale down his vision of a tree full of French dolls smoking cigars. This is Martin's formative experience: all his adult activities are in pursuit of greater and greater extravagance, denied him by his conservative Old World father.

Martin's success as a businessman is set in motion when he notices that Charley Stratemeyer, a day clerk at the Vanderlyn Hotel, walks to the Dressler shop each day for a cigar. The enterprising Martin offers to deliver the cigar on the condition that Stratemeyer will generate some word-of-mouth for the shop, since the cigars sold at the hotel newsstand have not been well marketed. Because of Martin's precocious perception of the basic elements of a consumer society—assessing the needs and desires of the consumer, finding the means of delivering the product or service, and advertising its availability—his future success seems assured. One day, in line with the narrative's connecting of business and sexuality, when Martin delivers the cigar,

Stratemeyer takes him upstairs, and the boy sees actors rehearsing. His eyes focus on a single detail that becomes fixed in his memory: at the end of a bed, a pair of feet, presumably female, one of which is "naked" (12).

Yet another formative experience is generated by the family's brief vacation each year in a seaside resort. If the Vanderlyn episode of the naked foot is associated with a hotel's mildly illicit nature, this resort hotel suggests a poor boy's delight in vacationing for three nights with his family. Like Otto Dressler's "extravagant" gesture of ensuring his wife has the piano he cannot easily afford, this vacation signals the father's susceptibility to "extravagance," given that the family travels to the sea by train. Martin has yet another "epiphanic" experience at the pier where the train line ends, but the world does not, for beyond the sea is England and a "world, immense and extravagant" (16).

At fourteen Martin begins his adult life by becoming a bellboy at the Vanderlyn. His father encourages him to take the job, over his mother's objection to his leaving school. The utter absence of reference to Martin's having been in school suggests its unimportance to him. It also reminds us that this narrative is a fable in which what is in the fable is enhanced by what is omitted. Readers sense that Martin will rise in the hotel staff because he is hard-working, conscientious, and eager to please. Additionally the narrative indicates "Otto wanted him to have the chance to better himself" (20). As though Martin were the son Willy Loman in Arthur Miller's *Death of a Salesman* wants to produce, the boy *knows* people "like" him and "have their eye on him," especially females, from young girls to the elderly. Martin notes their smiles as tokens of his ability to anticipate their desires. As the object of their "gaze," Martin, like Willy Loman, knows that success depends on the ability to "sell" himself.

When Martin is fifteen, this perception is confirmed in a bizarre episode that climaxes his apprenticeship in the hotel world. Martin becomes the "special" bellboy to Mrs. Louise Hamilton, described as "buxom bustling handsome," a lady, whose salient feature is her "large black eyes" (27). Parked in the hotel by her businessman-husband, Mrs. Hamilton expresses frustration through nonstop dissatisfaction with the hotel's service. Clearly she feels she is getting no "satisfaction," and tests Martin's ability to provide it when a cold develops into a fever. Eventually the "room service" Martin is called upon to provide leads to a precipitous drop in her complaints about the hotel. The viewpoint in the climactic scene is the innocent Martin's. He "enter[s] her fever-dream, at first awkwardly, then easily," and experiences "a sudden warm wet sinking and sinking" (32). After the Hamiltons leave, Henning the assistant manager informs the boy that "Mrs. Hamilton had commended Martin to him" (33). It scarcely seems coincidental that the next chapter begins with Henning's calling Martin into his office to offer him a phallic *cigar* and a promotion to desk clerk, telling the boy, "We've been keeping an eye on you" (34), especially after Mrs. Hamilton had more than "an eye" on him.

His new position has two major consequences for Martin, apparently different but ultimately interconnected. Martin has the confidence and the money to take over the Vanderlyn's tobacco stand and hire Bill Baer to staff it, making this his first "business venture." As desk clerk, Martin also is responsible for "keeping an eye" on the lobby. That surveillance eventually includes the request of Mrs. Margaret Bell, yet another "handsome woman," to look after her ten-year-old daughter while she is out. To his embarrassment, Martin discovers "Little Alice" also has her eye on him, develops a crush, and unsettles him with her gifts of a lock of golden hair and then a locket with her picture. One day when Mrs. Bell is late, Martin becomes angry and his hand inadvertently falls on Alice's shoulder, causing her "startled, almost violent look" and his "inner bursting."

The upshot of the quasi-sexual encounter with blatantly "underage" Alice is another epiphanic moment for Martin, who sees the lobby's women shedding their clothes in sexual abandon. The "terror" he experiences represents his vision of female sexuality as a menacing contagion, potential in the innocent Alice's crush on him, and earlier in Louise Hamilton's seduction. Clearly sexuality must be cordoned off from the potential rise in his professional life, and it is hardly coincidental that, after the Bells leave, Martin seeks out the prostitutes of West Twenty-fifth and Sixth Avenue with the somewhat older Bill Baer as guide. That being done, Martin is ready to be called in by Mr. Westerhoven, the manager, and offered a job as his personal secretary at double his salary. Even more important to his future than the money is the initiation into hotel management through on-the-job training. Martin is quickly learning how to manage his professional and sex lives.

Having grasped this "management skill," Martin is primed for success. A larger salary and increased profits from the tobacco stand generate "resources" for Martin to invest. At twenty, when today's undergraduates are likely to be just beginning courses in their business major, Martin buys and renovates the "Paradise Musée," a dilapidated wax-figures museum, to open the first in what will become a chain of lunchrooms, a forerunner of fast-food restaurants. When the museum's owner treats him as a boy, too young to start a business, Martin turns to the hotel's chief engineer, Walter Dundee, who will become his partner. Eventually Dundee also becomes his only good friend, after Bill Baer rejects the promotion to manage the lunchroom. If Martin represents the adventure of dreaming oneself into a larger being, Bill reminds him of his father and all those who lack the courage to follow their dreams.

Readers can readily see why this novel was tapped for the Pulitzer Prize for the best *American* novel in 1997. If Millhauser's preceding novel, *From the Realm of Morpheus,* pushed the limits of the traditional novel, *Martin Dressler* settles readers into a novel that could not be more "American," and attracts its readership with a modern success story. The first lunchroom whets Martin's appetite for the next, and like the renovating of the antiquated "Musée" to become a modern lunchroom, it directs Martin's attention to bringing the Vanderlyn into the modern age. Martin is a forerunner of the twentieth-century entrepreneur in his brilliant perception of what the public wants: in this case, both the architecture and furnishings of the Old World and the conveniences of the modern. Lying in his "boyhood bed," Martin thrills to the modern world's "dynamos and electric lights," speaking to his restless impulse to bring about modern improvements. He likens himself to a powerful locomotive on the elevated tracks above the city, thrusting its way into the future.

To mark the next "expansion" of his being, Martin rents an apartment in the Bellingham Hotel in the Upper West Side, still almost a rural address. Tellingly the Bellingham has "medieval turrets" and "modern hydraulic elevators," a potential model for the renovated Vanderlyn. Even more telling is Martin's connection with the three Vernon women with whom he will spend most evenings in the lobby's parlor. Martin will eventually "marry" the Vernon threesome, since each woman represents a different need in Martin. Mrs. Vernon is the mature, seductive woman he found attractive in Mrs. Hamilton and Mrs. Bell. The fatigued and passive, fair-haired Caroline is an older Alice Bell, or Poe's child-bride Annabel Lee. The dark-haired Emmeline is a friend, confidante, and business associate, who suffers his inability to read her pain in being asked to carry his marriage proposal to her sister.

Added to Martin's Vernon harem is the chambermaid Marie Haskova, whose friendship he never reveals to them, as though she were a "secret mistress." Like Dora, his first prostitute, or Gerda the Swede, Marie represents sexuality made available to him because of his money, class, and gender. Appropriately on his wedding night, after Caroline makes it clear she not only has no desire for him but does not even understand why a married couple sleeps together, he rushes to Marie, who silently welcomes him into her bed. Martin may return to the Bellingham and call on Mrs. Vernon to explain a wife's duties, but Caroline will never represent more than a passive body to him, a "marital device" for his gratification. The sterility of the marriage is troped by the absence of children, even though Martin forces himself on Caroline nightly for a time.

The psychology of Martin's relationships with women is clear. He *wants* a Marie or a Gerda, not an Emmeline a colleague, a "sister." It is difficult to decide how exactly he "wants" Caroline. When the narrative provides access to his consciousness, Martin is constructing her as a fairy-tale child bride he deludes himself into believing he could awaken, as the conventional Prince Charming awoke "Dornröschen," or Thorn-Rose, with a kiss. What he secretly wants is no *single* relationship with a woman to distract him from his romantic dreaming, but more importantly to sap the energy required by his imagination to turn his dreams into the "worlds" his chain of hotels will become. The lunchrooms were inevitably unsatisfying to his imagination. Martin is aware "his passion was for working things out, bringing things together, arranging the unarrangeable, making combinations" (123). Each was an added item in a series, rather than a more complex and intricate working out of his impulse to be a "world" maker, with each world richer and more complex than its predecessor. The narrative will turn the perverted notion of the "American dream" as the pursuit of obscene wealth inside out, restoring it as the earlier dream of remaking oneself psychologically, or even spiritually, in this New World, this second chance to regenerate the heart and soul of the human race.

That impulse to make worlds finds its outlet in ever larger and grander hotels, or apartment houses, so complete that residents never really need to go out. This new direction for his life work is troped as a dynamo in the darkness beneath the Vanderlyn, in whose lobby he has yet another vision of the immense force for change with which he aligns himself. The hotel into which he will remake the tired, old Vanderlyn is not so much a building he will "observe" as a structure he will "inhabit," as his spirit inhabits his body, "as if the structure *were* his own body" (174; emphasis added). It is hardly a coincidence that the first hotel he builds, after finishing the Vanderlyn's renovation, is called "The Dressler," and the next is "The New Dressler." If Otto Dressler is the old and fixed "body" of the past, Martin is energized by the power of endless self-transformation, ceaseless "bodybuilding," impelled by a spirit ever hungering for the new.

Martin himself conceptualizes each building as a "little world in itself," an "experimental" city, as a model for the city outside it (181). His hotels become department stores[2] as well because they are in "different forms the thrust toward vertical community that seemed to Martin the great fact of the modern city" (181). To actualize his vision of a hotel chain in which each new hotel transcends its predecessor, Martin turns to Harwinton, who exploits his training in psychology to market products and services in terms of perceived needs and desires.

Two other elements the architect Rudolf Arling builds into "The Dressler" for Martin are the museum and the amusement park. These are elements readers have encountered in Millhauser's shorter fiction such as "The Barnum Museum" and "Paradise Park." In their rudimentary form in "The Dressler," these elements are aimed at surprising and amusing; they are expressions of the need to escape the "monotonous regularity" in traditional hotels, which Martin believes he must avoid "like the plague." Hotel guests may be surprised to encounter phenomena such as "a circular theater in which a panorama of the entire Manhattan shoreline continually unwound" (212–13), or the "Pageant of Industry and invention, which contained working scale models of an Otis elevator, a steam crane lifting an I-beam" (213), and other expressions of modern technology. One apartment offers residents an artificial cave, containing four rooms and a waterfall; another has a forest with artificial trees and wild flowers. In the subterranean levels, guests and visitors encounter a theater district with actual theatrical productions.

These innovations will be extended in the New Dressler and the ultimate apartment hotel—the Grand Cosmo. What Martin and Arling designed in the first hotel as amusing departures from conventional apartments become in the New Dressler rooms offering guests/residents something approaching the theme park. Arling offers six different options for what Harwinton will advertise as "A Room with Vacation, Best Deal in the Nation" (237). These range from a campground in a pine forest, without pesky mosquitoes or marauding bears, or the deck of an ocean liner that unlike the *Titanic* is indeed unsinkable, to a whole national park with a "geyser, a waterfall, a glacier, a small canyon" (237). The venturesome might visit the Museum of Exotic Places in the hotel's subterranean realm, where they might find "the canals of Venice (with real water and gondolas)" or "the Amazon jungle . . . inhabited by actors in authentic costumes" (238), but presumably without headhunters or annoying crocodiles.

Meanwhile, Caroline is leaving Martin, and unfortunately for him taking Emmeline with her. Having refused to move into the New Dressler, Caroline begins to sleep in her sister's bed while Emmeline sleeps on the couch, like a husband who has misbehaved. Eventually Emmeline returns to her own bed and adopts the "husband" role—not sexually, of course—thrust upon her by the "feminine" Caroline. Martin becomes the "odd man out," having lost his "lover" Caroline, his colleague Emmeline, their seductive "mature" mother, and even Marie Haskova, who apparently got "renovated" out of the Bellingham Hotel, when it was demolished to make way for apartment houses. The women in his life who stimulated his entrepreneurial energies to imagine, to arrange, to construct the physical expressions of his American dreaming of transforming himself through the guise of each new richer and more "extravagant" hotel are now depleting his resources. There will be one last enterprise—the Grand Cosmo—the biggest manmade world in the cosmos itself, a world that even Martin himself knows will be the end of the world, the final extravaganza to stand up to the Old Man who might have snared his boy within a life in miniature, in the tiny, replicated Old Country of the Dressler tobacco shop.

Because Martin senses the Grand Cosmo will be his last effort to flaunt his obsession with extravagance, he and Arling pull out all the stops for a "world" to end all worlds. The tone here, as in other Millhauser stories, is difficult to determine with anything approaching certainty. It would be easy enough to misinterpret this novel as Millhauser's criticism of the self-immersed plutocrat, pursuing wealth and power,[3] but the narrative makes it clear that Martin cares little for money or the power it conventionally produces. In a sense he is an overgrown boy with an Erector set or a Lego box with a seemingly infinite number of pieces, building ever larger and more complicated and eventually more fantastic constructions to push engineering to its limits—the sort of high-level "play," or art of actualizing fantasy forms, evident in the Arab Emirate of Dubai.

Martin confronts the dilemma at the heart of tragedy, going back to Oedipus.[4] To survive, humans play it safe and resist the temptation to draw attention to themselves by threatening the gods, or the nature of things, with their impulse to overreach, to aspire to more than human limits allow. On the other hand, it is just such aspirations that celebrate our essential humanness—to strive forevermore, despite the risk of "punishment" for unwillingness to be satisfied with mere survival. As Martin begins to see his dream-palace, the Grand Cosmo, heading toward a debacle, commensurate with its aspirations, and threatening to pull down everything Martin has achieved, he *embraces* the catastrophe, as though the nature of things has finally shown him the limits, rather like the rebellious boy who secretly welcomes his father's "laying down the law."

Indeed, Otto Dressler figures largely in Martin's tragic fall. In a passage allowing access to Martin's consciousness, the narrative offers a view of his tragic effort to preserve agency in his fall. The Grand Cosmo debacle must be some "punishment." He accepts the notion of punishment, even though he cannot determine the "crime" for which he is being punished. The "crime" may have been marrying Caroline instead of Emmeline, perhaps even his exploitation of Marie Haskova on his wedding night. After Martin moves back to the tobacco shop, he recalls his father's slowness in expressing anger for his boy's "not stepping carefully enough among the cigar boxes" (281) in the shop window. The issues raised by this tragic fall become magnified toward cosmic proportions as Martin concedes that the construction of the Grand Cosmo amounted to "an act of disobedience" (281), and he finally grasps that the reason for his fall is "deeper than crime . . . a forbidden desire, the desire to create the world" (282). Thus Martin connects his fall with angering his father when he overreached himself by aspiring to improve the tobacco shop. He only sensed as a boy what he now *knows* as a man: only catastrophe can be the consequence of stirring the jealous anger of a Father who punishes sons when they attempt to arrogate to themselves the power to create worlds.

The difficulty some reviewers faced in reading *Martin Dressler* demonstrates the challenge of understanding Steven Millhauser without the fullest awareness gained by reading his entire oeuvre. Accordingly Martin Dressler is less accurately seen as a satire on the ambitious plutocrat of a century ago; instead Martin joins other overreachers such as August Eschenburg and Eisenheim the Illusionist. Surely Millhauser offers ample evidence of failure in these self-immersed pursuers of a world beyond limits. The Martin Dressler who, with Arling's assistance, creates fantastic living spaces, described by Millhauser's seemingly limitless detail and extensive examples, must be the recipient of the author's sympathetic engagement, for often Millhauser himself mimics Dressler's impulses by pushing the narrative beyond conventional limits, and demanding that his readers follow him into fantasy worlds whose realistic detail supports our notion of their "reality," at the same time a part of the reader's mind occasionally says, wait a minute, Mr. Millhauser, that just cannot be possible. And the author responds, perhaps, but that does not keep me from wanting to make it so.

In the end Martin associates his tragic fall from greatness with the falling of the snow, associating the fall of his hotel empire with the fading out of Marie Haskova, the Vernons, Walter Dundee, and the world itself. His acceptance of his fall bespeaks a quiet awareness that, beginning with the creation of the cigar tree, all the dreams he strove to construct had to inevitably fall. Martin is no Ahab shaking his fist at the heavens for defeating him. He seems secretly satisfied that this awareness of how all things fall would have been impossible without the vision of what might be constructed and the energy to attempt to actualize those "dreams." Like other tragic figures, Martin understands it is our greatness as humans to defy limitations, even though those who are defiant inevitably pay the price for that defiance, and it is a price they are willing to pay because it certifies the power of human dreams to transcend the comfortable boundaries of conventionality.

CHAPTER 9

The Knife Thrower and Other Stories

In the range of its subjects and its approaches to fiction, *The Knife Thrower and Other Stories* (1999) offers a collection of stories that the author's readers will identify as "classic Millhauser." The collection brings together a dozen stories providing a cornucopia of what Millhauser had been publishing in magazines for over a decade. *The Knife Thrower,* for example, contains his first published story, "The New Automaton Theater," omitted from *In the Penny Arcade* because "August Eschenburg" also focused on automaton-making. The presence of "The New Automaton Theater" in this later collection highlights the more sophisticated and often deeper representations of approaches and perceptions readers of Millhauser have become accustomed to.

The opening story, "The Knife Thrower," for example, offers a figure that fascinates Millhauser—the "popular-culture" entertainer, with a touch of the artist. Hensch, the knife thrower, like Eisenheim, the illusionist, known only by his surname, brings into the small, central European city of the narrator a powerful mystique of the "other," the alien who excites his audience with his dangerous "art." Like those who attend auto races, Hensch's audience is titillated by the potential accident that could injure, even kill the attractive, scantily clad woman he throws his knives at, providing an opportunity for the male gaze. The act follows the conventional "climax" rhythm of ever-more daring and dangerous challenges to Hensch's skill in ensuring that the knife lands exactly where he intends it to, and where viewers know they *should want it to,* even though they also sense the appeal of that fugitive, subversive impulse to see some blood flowing.

The narrative masterfully plays on readers' expectations of where the plot is leading them, or more specifically how the story will end. The action appears to move toward its climax with the increasingly subtle demonstrations of Hensch's art, namely, the incorporation of blood-letting into the performance as the knife thrower succeeds in producing closer "misses," or "flesh wounds," as he just pierces the woman's skin. The next seemingly logical movement, marked by the reappearance of Hensch's assistant in a long, black dress, is audience participation. First Susan Parker is positioned at the partition to receive a "memento" of the performance, then Thomas, whose memento will be the scar of a knife through his hand. As readers lean forward in anticipation of an even more dramatic climax to Hensch's performance—and Millhauser's—the story takes a bizarre turn toward the macabre. When Hensch's female assistant announces, "And now I must say we have time for only one more event, this evening," and calls for a volunteer to make "the ultimate sacrifice" (*The Knife Thrower* 12), suspense builds for the audience, and for readers because "ultimate sacrifice" smacks of battlefield heroism—say, a soldier's throwing himself on a live grenade to save the lives of his buddies.

Unlike the story's earlier style with its precise, detailed descriptions of the knife thrower's art, the finale of the performance is less clear and definite. The assistant leads the "girl" who has volunteered to the partition, cheerily asks the volunteer's name, and tells Laura she "must be very brave" (13). The narrating "we" expresses confusion and a feeling he/they ought to demand an explanation, but events quickly move beyond anyone's ability to be anything but a passive witness to this "ultimate sacrifice," punctuated by the woman's cry and no sound of the knife hitting wood. Hensch acknowledges the audience with a bow, and the curtain falls. What are we to make of this bizarre open ending?

The narrator notes that the viewers respond in diverse ways, most of them expressed ironically. The knife thrower "justified his reputation" or "had the right to develop his art," or the "final act had probably been a set-up, the girl had probably leaped smiling to her feet" (14) after the curtain came down. The narrator generalizes, "when all was said and done . . . the knife thrower had gone too far" (14). Beneath these mundane, conventional sentiments, readers sense the audience is in denial that a girl may have been murdered before their very eyes.

The absence of a clear ending is a clue to the narrative's focus. Our concern is more properly with the "middle" than the ending, with the experience of finding ourselves in a nightmare of dramatically increasing injury and suffering, witnessed by a group in which no one stands up and shouts, "This must stop!" Perhaps this approach sounds too morally righteous, in line with Edmund Burke's dictum, "All that is necessary for the triumph of evil is that good men do nothing." Valid as Burke's assertion might be, the narrative communicates what most have felt: the helplessness within a group, silently witnessing violence.

This macabre "final act" in "Knife Thrower" provides a segue to the next story, "The Visit." Readers are likely to remember this brief story the longest. It begins straightforwardly in a situation familiar to many. After not having heard from his "best friend" Albert in nine years, the narrator receives an invitation, virtually a *demand,* to pay Albert and his wife a visit at their country home. Noting that Albert has lost none of his domineering style, the narrator sets out, hoping to have time with his friend to catch up on their lives since they last saw each other.

Part of the undeveloped situation is also the narrator's curiosity about his friend's wife, another a situation we can relate to. What will she be like, and how will her presence affect the friends' reunion? When the two men have reacquainted themselves and gone inside so the narrator can meet Albert's wife, readers discover it will have to be Albert who fixes lunch because his wife Alice cannot. She is a two-foot-tall frog, who apparently came with the property. After lunch, Alice accompanies the two men on their tour of the "estate" and joins them for dinner. Eventually the narrator notes Alice giving Albert the eye, indicating she wants to take him to bed. Because it is early and he is not ready to turn in, the narrator finishes the wine, trying to avoid "petty and cruel" thoughts about "frog love."

The next morning, after a wretched night of insomnia and bad dreams, the narrator focuses on Albert working in the yard with Alice keeping him company. Surprisingly the narrator witnesses something like real love in the couple, "a mysterious rhythm trembling between Albert and his wife, a kind of lightness or buoyancy, a quivering sunlit harmony" (28), something the narrator has never experienced. As the narrator drives away, the substantiality of the house, its occupants, and the visit itself fade into the countryside, leaving the narrator, and readers, with the impression they have paid a visit to a bizarre but unforgettably real world, and as they drove away, pondering: did that really happen, or did I dream it?

These two visits to the "Twilight Zone" are followed by three others, moving the collection into further indeterminacy. "The Sisterhood of Night,"[1] with its clear connections to a similar sequence in the novella/novel *Enchanted Night,* recalls the first-person-plural voice of "The Knife Thrower" and that story's ending with its indefinite resolution of what went on in the "final act." Here the central question is: was Emily Gehring's confession a truthful revelation of a powerful, secret girl-gang involved in homoerotic activity on summer nights, or was Emily motivated by revenge against an innocent sorority of young women, forced to expel her for breaking the group's pledge of silence? Readers can only speculate where the truth lies.

Harter, the viewpoint character in "The Way Out," recalls the narrator of "The Visit." He too enters a world whose rules he would never have expected. Literally having just ended an affair with Martha, Harter looks up from re-donning his clothes as Martha's "little" husband opens the bedroom door, hisses to his "shamed" wife he will deal with her later, and tells Harter he can expect to hear from him. But Harter hears from him only through two men who visit and eventually drive him into the country, where the "little" husband is waiting for the "large soft man with broad, round shoulders and a boyish face" who has wronged him. Suddenly readers discover, as does Harter, that the two men have brought him to an early morning duel so Martha's husband can gain satisfaction for the violation of his marriage bed. Harter is so incredulous at stumbling into a duel that he is encouraged to see it all as a huge practical joke about which suddenly everyone will start laughing. He throws the gun away, and the story ends with these images of his final impressions: "his chest itched, somewhere a train was roaring, hundreds of yellow butterflies were beating their wings like mad" (65), subtly suggesting that Martha's husband was a good shot.

Rounding out this quintet of bizarre tales, "Flying Carpets" clearly moves us into a more conventional world of fantasy. The "flying carpets" seem to generate themselves out of a dominant element in Millhauser's earlier fiction —the crushing boredom and exquisite tedium of summer for young students two generations ago. This is the world of the first two novels in which the author functions as an archaeologist of an era, pre-television and well before the age of electronics, video games, social networking, and so forth. Here Millhauser adeptly uses a first-person point of view to ground the fantastic within the all-too-real world of a boy who readers can believe would be so overwhelmed by sweltering heat and boredom as to conjure up flying carpets to transport him to a world of freedom and excitement. It is no coincidence that these flying carpets have their origins in the exotic "Oriental" world of the Middle East, the "Araby" that James Joyce's narrator in the *Dubliners* story calls up to free himself from the dull prison-house of Dublin. Eventually summer ends, and the carpet is left to collect dust, as the academic New Year begins with another return to school.

"The New Automaton Theater" seems less a story than an essay with Heinrich Graum as an example of a master automaton-maker. It takes place in a Central European, German-speaking city, unidentified by the narrator, who speaks for the "we" of that city and their "devotion, which some call obsession" (76), with dramatic performances of clockwork figures. As in "The

Knife Thrower," Millhauser's use of first-person-plural viewpoint gives the impression of a whole group's responses to a popular form of entertainment.

The establishment of an authentic world is particularly important when the narrative occasionally taxes its readers' willingness to believe. Early on, for example, the narrative moves into a Millhauser "obsession"—miniatures.[2] Introducing the city's fascination with miniatures, the narrator generalizes: "No home is without its cherrystone basket, its peachpit troll" (77–78). Then readers are taken into the city museum's Hall of Miniatures, where they are asked to believe in incredible marvels of miniaturization such as "an ark carved from the pit of a cherry, containing three dozen pairs of clearly distinguishable animals, as well as Noah and his sons" (78), and other stretches of feasibility, reminiscent of the miniature of a miniature of the palace in the story "Cathay."

These efforts to force readers into stretching their capacity to believe in the incredible are not gratuitous, however. They are a prelude to the narrator's more serious attempt to lead readers into the fundamental principle in the history of automaton-making. This principle is "an ever-increasing mastery of the illusion of life" (78), the principle which energized August Eschenburg's pursuit of mechanical movement, indistinguishable from the movement of human muscles. Here the narrator is moving us toward the final challenge to credibility, as indicated by cleverly intruding the phrase "the clockwork souls" in describing the city's automatons.

The story is basically encouraging readers to accept the connection between the mechanical and the spiritual. As the mechanical representation of human motion achieves the illusion of being the equivalent of what the eye perceives as human movement, the automaton succeeds in advancing beyond the actual to new potentials for the human spirit. When the art of the automaton-maker can produce faces capable of expressing the subtlest of human emotions, it becomes conceivable that the automaton face can take another step beyond to achieve the representation of emotions the human face lacks the "mechanics" to express: "these finely wrought creatures are capable of expressing in their faces certain deep and complex emotions which the limited human musculature can never hope to achieve" (79). Readers are asked "to consider the relation between the physical and the spiritual, and to ask themselves whether the most poetic feeling in the soul of man can exist without the prosaic agency of a nervous system" (79). Accordingly the apparently frivolous term "clockwork souls" is revelatory of the possibility of a spiritual dimension in the mechanical.

If this art is by its very nature "mimetic," or "illusionistic," in its effort to represent "life," the narrator would dismiss the notion of a limited "realism" in favor of a "realism of means, which in no way excludes the fanciful" (79). The Automaton Theater for children has dragons, but they are "real dragons": "The real is used to bring forth the unreal. It is a mimesis of the fantastic, a scrupulous rendering of creatures who differ from real creatures solely by their quality of inexistence" (80). At the same time, the realism of the automatons' illusionist representation is limited by their size—merely six inches tall, in contrast to Count Orsini's life-sized automatons, which audiences laughed off the stage. The futile effort to make automatons the size of humans paradoxically punctures the mimetic pursuit of the human, which requires miniaturization.

In this way the pleasure of the automaton-maker's mastery of illusion is matched by its antithesis, the awareness of the real. Alternately it might be said the pleasure of mimesis is twofold. That is, the pleasure in mimesis has a second half that delights in discovering the limits of illusion, the ways in which imitation fails to represent everything. Indeed the more successful the creation of illusion, the more powerful the discovery of its limits is likely to be. Thus, unlike the child entirely captured by the illusion of reality in the theater, adult viewers may move into the illusion temporarily or partially, while also knowing it is an actor they are watching, not Hamlet.

Having established this context of automaton theater, the narrator moves into something more like a conventional narrative of a master automaton-maker, Heinrich Graum. Like August Eschenburg and other masters, Graum had a watchmaker-father, but little Heinrich was apprenticed at five to Rudolf Eisenmann ("Ironman"), whose workshop turned out many masters of automaton-making. In the midst of successful illusion-making, Millhauser himself discloses the "second pleasure" of mimesis by intruding a challenge to the reader's ability to believe. Young Heinrich was no child prodigy, we are told, but at seven he produced a "one-inch nightingale capable of sixty-four motions, including thirty-six separate motions of the head, and exhibiting such perfect craftsmanship that it was used in the orchard scene of Eisenmann's *Der Reisende Kavalier* ['The Traveling Cavalier']" (83). Alert readers are likely to wonder what Heinrich might have had to produce to qualify as a *prodigy.* Actually the narrator is making a point of denying Graum prodigy-status because as in other arts often the "prodigy of seven is the mediocrity of fifteen" (85).

Prodigy status is revealed in Heinrich's later childhood—ten to twelve—when he focuses on Eisenmann's masterpiece, the "famous magician." In eight months Heinrich could duplicate his master's "magician," licensing the apprentice to produce his first original work. Heinrich created a pianist who could play the "entire first movement of the Moonlight Sonata" (85) of

Beethoven—about four and a half minutes. His lack of musical background limited the pianist's movements, but the hands themselves signaled a "future master."

After spending six years studying the faces of automatons, Heinrich reveals greater promise. In "two feverish months" he produces his next figure, "Fraulein Elise," pronounced a "masterpiece" by Eisenmann. Five inches tall, the pubescent girl moves for twelve minutes: "Her famous walk, so indolently sensual, would alone have ensured the young master a place in the histories" (86). However, it is the "startling expressivity of the face" which allows access to "the very soul of this girl" (86). Heinrich's accomplishment was surprising because he had never been in love. After observing her twelve-minute performance over and over, an eighteen-year-old apprentice fell in love with Elise, thereby crediting the massive power of mimesis to encourage the lover to believe the automaton "real." "Fraulein Elise" demonstrates Heinrich's mastery of the traditional Automaton Theater's promise of expressing "mechanically" those spiritual states that human musculature cannot express.

As the outstanding automaton-maker of his time, Graum generates intense excitement each time a new creation is announced. Then at thirty-six he "suddenly fell silent" (89). After closing his theater, he vegetated for ten years before he began again. The "New Automaton Theater" opened with great excitement, but the first performance brought reactions ranging from anger to sickness and shame. What made these creations "new" was the deliberate effort to produce clumsiness, gracelessness, and ugliness—a foregrounding of these automatons *as automatons*.

Graum had taken mimesis to its logical extreme to represent the "reality" of automaton-ness. Their very clumsiness is artfully executed. Their motions are reduced, but in a manner creating a "particular rhythm" only the connoisseur can see, allowing these automatons to be "profoundly expressive in their own disturbing way, with motions never seen in automatons before." By forcing the audience to focus on the automatons per se, Graum has encouraged them "to share the emotions of automatons themselves" (93). Furthermore, just as the earlier automatons have the souls of humans, the new automatons have the "souls of clockwork creatures, grown conscious of themselves" (94). They are not replicas or imitations of anything, but a "new race" (94).

These new automatons have become particularly attractive to younger viewers, drawn to the pathos of their clumsy motions and the "inhuman longings" (94) of their "clockwork souls" (78). Their obsessive attraction to these automatons bespeaks a desire to enter the darkness of their souls and to feel unnamable emotions. "The new art is not a gentle art; its beauties are of an almost unbearable intensity" (95). Although the old art still flourishes, its "brilliant imitations seem to us nothing but clockwork confections" (96), while the new art draws viewers back by changing their dreams. Whether "decadence" or the "deepest and darkest flowering" of our art, "nothing can ever be the same" (96).

Despite its difficulties, this story rewards reading and rereading. In his *New York Times* review, Patrick McGrath called it "perhaps the strongest story in the collection, one that reminds us that in his exploration of the complicated responses we have to the products and projections of our own minds, Millhauser is without equal among contemporary writers."[3]

"Clair de Lune," with its moonlit summer world, is yet another expression of Millhauser's investment in the night-world. *Enchanted Night* and scenes from *Portrait of a Romantic* come readily to mind. Unlike the stories before and after, told in the "we," or first-person plural, "Clair de Lune" offers a first-person-singular narrative. The narrator is a fifteen-year-old boy, turned into an insomniac by many nights of inescapable moonlight—and because he is an adolescent.

First-person narrative and the eerie, moonlit setting support the story as fantasy, well before the boy walks on air. The narrator relates his moonlit adventure of playing wiffle-ball with four female classmates, particularly Sonja, on whose calves swinging in the moonlight he obsessively focuses while she sits on her kitchen counter. She exposes awareness of his male gaze by laughing, and when he asks why, she responds, "'Oh, nothing. . . . Everything. You, for example'" (104). Tellingly when Sonja adds: "'Let's call it a night, gang,'" the narrator notes that Marcia "seemed to be lifting her breasts towards the blue night sky, the summer moon" (104). Obviously the boy is stimulated and expectant. When she addresses him as "'Fair Knight,'" and "with a little mock curtsy" bids him "'farewell,' before pushing him out the door," the boy notes: "I saw her arm rise and felt her fingers touch my face" (104).

This is the point at which this boy from an earlier time in America[4] joins Danny in *Enchanted Night* as one enamored of the night. After Sonja closes the door behind him, the boy feels transformed by the moonlight, which dissolves the "day-world" and produces in him a "new lightness" (105). He becomes aware of an "odd buoyancy," which at first lifts his feet a few inches off the sidewalk but eventually wafts him away "into the blue countries of the night" (106), suggesting the transformation wrought by incipient love.

The title of "The Dream of the Consortium" has a nice ambivalence. The consortium has an extraordinary dreamlike ambition to transform the old, familiar "emporium" into a modern superstore. The first-person-plural narration is especially appropriate because "we" represent a community of shoppers, dreaming of a store to surprise customers with immense offerings. "We" sound quite young, but consumer culture infantilizes us, pandering to our desire for everything we want and secretly believe we *deserve:* if I buy enough extravagant and expensive *things,* I will achieve the happiness I deserve, given the wonderful person I am.

The impulse here is gigantism, another variety of overreaching. This is the "Texas" mentality: if it is the biggest, it's the best. Indeed this superstore has a catalog department allowing customers to order replicas of the Parthenon, the Colosseum, or a Roman aqueduct. Recently a Texas oilman ordered a Colosseum for his ranch, but most orders are placed by corporations: "a software company in New Mexico had recently ordered the Baths of Caracalla and Hadrian's Villa . . . , and another firm in southern California had ordered the entire Acropolis" (115). Selling replicas has expanded into substitute travel-experiences, generated from anger over billions of Americans dollars lost to tourism abroad. States such as Texas or Montana can now purchase reproductions of European villages, keeping dollars here and reducing the discomforts of foreign travel.

The superstore has everything customers could imagine—and more. The departments on the nineteen stories and four basement levels are full of *things* to feed the shopper's appetite for self-indulgence, "from sequined evening gowns and chauffeur's livery to jeweled chess sets and imported jade palace dogs from the Imperial Palace of Beijing" (114). The store's designers dramatically juxtapose departments, allowing customers to experience the thrill of moving from lingerie to refrigerators. Customers are also psychologically conditioned to feel overwhelmed through curving aisles to give the illusion of no end to the wares.

The effect of reading this bizarre story replicates the experience of the shopper, overwhelmed by the complex organization of the store's—and the story's—endless details. So great is the department store's impact that upon leaving its shoppers "have the absurd sensation that [they] have entered still another department, composed of ingeniously lifelike streets" (124). The illusion of this fabricated "world" makes it difficult for shoppers to believe in a reality that is anything but shopping and consumerism. And that may be the point of the story.

"Balloon Flight, 1870" offers an analog to "Flying Carpets," but in the "real" world of French soldiers doing aerial reconnaissance in the Franco-Prussian War. First-person-singular viewpoint effectively offers the sense of wonder in early flight, before the "I" experiences a "terrible indifference" in which "there's no difference between Paris and Berlin; between Paris and pissing" (129). Although surviving the descent from the "too-high heavens" to the "human turmoil" (136) below, he has been irrevocably changed by the flight.

Set in a fictional amusement park of a century ago, "Paradise Park" offers an analog in popular entertainment to "The Dream of the Consortium" in its "flamboyance or excess" (137). Here the excess involves the sating of the consumer's appetite for diverse and intense forms of excitement. One significant similarity to the superstore is the strategy of verticalism, of stretching upward toward the heavens, rather than outward on the horizontal plane. The "vertical thrust" is better justified here by the competition for space, given that Paradise Park is an ocean-front establishment.

A salient feature of the park is its "four-hundred-feet high white wall" (137), allowing visitors to locate it miles away and adding the aura of secrecy to the park's "allure." This secrecy is enhanced by reducing access to two entries. Even the entry facing the ocean offers no immediate view of the park's immense interior since it too affords access only through a tunnel.

From the outset the story foregrounds the park's fundamental purpose—to improvise exciting, new forms of entertainment not for themselves, but to make money. We learn that "a single ride called the Sidewinder, which cost $86,000 to build, drew $375,000 in receipts in the first three seasons" (140), an impressive profit in a dollar worth $20 today. Unlike "rides," Charles Sarabee, the owner, devises "Adventures." For a dime, visitors "could enter the Dark Forest and be attacked by a gang of bandits, or step into the Streets of Lisbon and experience the famous earthquake" (141). Because this story is set in Millhauser World, the big attraction is a miniature of the whole park, making Paradise Park seem all the more immense and complex to the entrant. Sarabee is aware his biggest challenge is boredom, making him ceaselessly innovative in engineering new "products" for the amusement consumer. Therein lay the great potential for failure, as ever-more grandiose and experimental projects tapped into the impulse to overreach that ultimately doomed Martin Dressler as a hotel tycoon. Millhauser seems to be asking: how does the entrepreneur, the inventor, the artist, or more specifically the writer, avoid something like the hubris at the heart of ancient Greek tragedy? At the pinnacle of success, Sarabee decides to reinvent his business as a "NEW PARADISE PARK: *You Have to See It to Believe It*" (149).

This "NPP" is the first in a string of major innovations to offer the "next thing" in an amusement park endlessly reinventing itself. The "NPP" is constructed under the existing Paradise Park, yet another evidence of Millhauser's interest in underground spaces. As a savvy entrepreneur, Sarabee anticipates visitors feeling cheated if the subterranean park were exactly the same, and so the "NPP" has entirely new rides, drawing visitors into a carnival spirit produced by the excesses of these rides. Including movie and vaudeville theaters for the first time, the "NPP" was a success, but some saw Sarabee as overstepping the bounds of amusement parks and encouraging visitors to dismiss traditional elements, ultimately leaving visitors unsatisfied, and restless.

Not surprisingly, Sarabee goes even farther, obsessed with taking the "amusement park to its farthest limit of expression" (154). Two years in the making, yet another "new" park opens on a second underground level with even more manic expressions of Sarabee's dreams. Visitors now can ride on a spherical Ferris wheel, or experience even more extreme "Adventures." They can, for example, feel what being buried alive is like, or enter a seraglio with six hundred concubines, or "witness the demonic possession of the girls at the witch trials of Salem" (155). Despite its success, Sarabee is already secretly planning the next park.

Moving toward fantasy, this park, "Sarabee's Folly," is abandoned in hopes its limitations could be "remedied" in the next version. The reinventions of "Paradise Park" begin coming so fast that readers may lose track of which is which. Critics celebrated this one as an artistic masterpiece or as an invention making Sarabee the "Edison of amusement-park impresarios" (162). Plummeting ticket sales sealed its failure, however, and another reinvention —this time more blatantly sinister—was planned. Dubbed the "Devil's Park" for its "Lover's Leap," "Suicide Coaster," and similar features, it was a popular success—like Hausenstein's pornographic automaton theater—but condemned by outraged critics. Sarabee and his ultimate park went up in flames, a suspected suicidal embrace of his final creation.

As Millhauser leads readers through "Paradise Park," he too is constructing his own ever-more complicated and extreme "amusements." Descriptions become more mysterious and fantastic. Not coincidentally this story is the collection's longest, stretching toward novella length. In its manic pursuit of excess, it seems like a compressed version of *Martin Dressler*.[5] Millhauser knows his creations' tendency to overreach, and many would agree "Paradise Park" could not have lasted any longer.

Much as the immensity and dark power of "Paradise Park" make it seem the real end of this collection, two stories remain—"miniatures" in contrast to the manic energy of "Paradise Park." "Kaspar Hauser Speaks" offers the monologue of an early nineteenth-century European sensation with his stories of a bizarre childhood, growing up alone in a dark dungeon, a feral child who had to learn to be human as a young adult. Well after he died at twenty-one, Hauser remained an enigma. Millhauser's choice of first-person narrative could not be more appropriate, for it underscores how little is known beyond what Hauser alleged to be his history.

"Beneath the Cellars of Our Town" offers a final expression of first-person-plural narration here, no less difficult to believe, despite the "we" the narrator speaks for. As a tie-in with "Paradise Park," this town has an underground world of tunnels through which the townspeople move as comfortably as above. Readers may wonder if the story seeks to posit a hidden element of community life, that is, the town's secret, invisible life, on the analogy of our difficulty in knowing the real person behind the public persona. However, the story may also be another corner of the Millhauser world in which a seemingly ordinary expression of the real world opens out to potential fantasy.

CHAPTER 10

Enchanted Night: A Novella

Enchanted Night is unique among Steven Millhauser's novellas. Unlike the three in *Little Kingdoms* or in *The King in the Tree, Enchanted Night* is the only novella Millhauser has published by itself. At one hundred pages *Enchanted Night* is about the size of "The Little Kingdom of J. Franklin Payne," one of three novellas in *Little Kingdoms.* As with the 1997 reprinting of *The Barnum Museum* (1990) by Dalkey Archive Press, Crown's decision to publish *Enchanted Night* as a separate novella offers testimony to the collateral value of Millhauser's winning the Pulitzer Prize for *Martin Dressler* in 1997.

Although not perhaps unique to this novella, *Enchanted Night* distinguishes itself from the others in its highly lyrical or musical elements. In his March 2003 *Transatlantica* interview with Marc Chénetier, Millhauser himself spoke of how "the conception of the work was musical—a theme and variations on a summer night." He goes on to explain the relevance of the epigraph from Ben Jonson's 1603 poem "Hymn to Diana" in the lines

> Lay thy bow of pearl apart
> and thy crystal-shining quiver.
> Give unto the flying hart
> Space to breathe, how short soever.

These lines indicate that, "in *Enchanted Night,* I gave the flying hart—the restless heart—a little space to breathe. Day will come soon enough."

At this novella's center is yet another of Millhauser's expressions of his own enchantment with the night.[1] In reading this narrative, taking place on a single summer night, readers are reminded of how much of the first two novels was comprised of night scenes. In the Chénetier interview the novelist says that "art is connected in my mind—in my body—with a sense of enhancement, of radical pleasure, of affirmation, of revelry. Darkness is the element against which this deeper force asserts itself. It may even be that this force deliberately seeks out darkness, in order to assert itself more radically." In the novella "Franklin Payne," it is no coincidence that Payne drafts his animations at night nor that even after color has become possible he insists on continuing to do black-and-white drawings because he sees them as intrinsic to the art of animation.

Enchanted Night is unique on yet another score. Unlike the other novellas, *Enchanted Night* resembles a collection of stories whose narrative threads or "plots" are interrupted by each other. The "plot" of numerous "characters" out on this summer night is rendered through narrative units of widely differing length, with titles of varying pertinence. Although readers may be willing to take each section as a vignette, or discrete expression of a moonlit summer night's impact on those who are outdoors, it is natural for some readers to anticipate the novella's disclosure of connections among these figures of the night.

The time setting also defines *Enchanted Night.* This is *one* "enchanted night," and because the season is summer it is a short "night," the narrative occurring between midnight and dawn about 5:00 A.M. This time compression contributes a sense of urgency. If the narrative is to offer some "sense of an ending," there is little time to do it. Additionally the shortened time-span raises the issue of genre once again: How does a novella differ from a short story or novel other than in its length? How dependent is the novella on communicating a sense of a reasonably developed action with some resolution?

Yet another element of the time setting deserves attention. Once again we are in Millhauser Country, the small-town America of the author's childhood in southern Connecticut. This novella deliberately leaves the time vague in an effort to capture a summer night's essence. There *are* some clues that the year might be sometime in the 1950s. The setting seems not to be the 1930s or '40s, with the impact of first the Depression and later World War II. And it is not the '60s or '70s with their cultural upheaval, evident even in rural America. Additionally these people are outdoors in part because indoors is hot, given that even window air conditioners for bedrooms are not yet in general use. Finally the narrative suggests the '50s in the inklings of looming cultural change within the postwar "good times" of that era. One indication of a darker underside is the figures of Smitty and Blake as amusing expressions of a '50s "menace," more immediate than the "Red menace"—"juvenile delinquency." And there are "girl gangs," suggesting an earlier society still patriarchal enough to be surprised by teenaged girls who "act out" of their traditional images as "sweet young things."

A final distinction in *Enchanted Night* is that its "characters" range across a broad spectrum. At one end, the narrative includes conventional characters such as Laura, Haverstraw, Danny, Mrs. Kasco, Coop,[2] and Peggy. However, there are also non-human figures such as a store-window mannequin; the dolls in the attic who awake at night, reminding us of the dolls in Payne's animated film; stock figures such as Pierrot and his fickle girlfriend Columbine, the nature god Pan, and preeminently Diana the moon-goddess. Also included are less fully developed characters such as the unnamed "woman who lives alone," who refuses to acknowledge she has been the victim of a home invasion by the girl gang and invites them to stay for lemonade. Or the girls themselves who have gang names such as "Summer Storm" and "Black Star" to conceal their identities. The presence of the mannequin and dolls may make even human characters such as the "woman" and girl-gang members seem like statues similar to Michelangelo's "Dying Slave," a human figure apparently struggling to escape its marble block and achieve fuller development.[3] And conversely the moonlight and Coop's slightly inebriated but adoring gaze animates the mannequin, allowing her to move in the store window and express human feelings.

Of the more conventional characters, Laura Engstrom is among the most central, partly because she is the first to be introduced. At fourteen, she is "restless," confined to her home and family, bored, desiring some excitement, uneasy about her adolescent body and not wanting it seen. She "has to get out of the house" and ends up in a spruce grove where she strips to moonbathe. Unfortunately she falls asleep and awakes to find herself the object of a sexual predator's gaze—he is identified only as the "man with shiny black hair" (*Enchanted Night* 40). The situation is tense because readers have witnessed him stalking girls in the library, where he seemed satisfied to merely gaze, but Laura is totally nude.

Laura's rescuer is the middle-aged Haverstraw, probably the novella's most complex character. Haverstraw (no given name) lives with/off his widowed mother, and is working on an "immense project, an experiment in memory, which will justify him" (11).[4] As he has many evenings before, he has visited his friend Mrs. Kasco, the mother of a high-school friend, to discuss books and ideas. After Haverstraw's friend moved with his father to Mexico, Mrs. Kasco considered having an affair with Haverstraw, encouraging readers to anticipate a romance between these two loners on this "enchanted night." Actually, an affair is no more likely than Coop's consummating his "love" for the store-window mannequin.

Haverstraw's encounter with Laura's stalker seems a turning point in his life. When Haverstraw brandishes the heavy novel, Theodore Dreiser's *Jenny Gerhardt* loaned him by Mrs. Kasco, the stalker flees, without having seen Laura, or so Haverstraw attempts to reassure her. His back turned, he tosses Laura his windbreaker, and as a token of her gratitude for his kindness, she leaves a partial roll of Life Savers. His final section reveals a Haverstraw with renewed faith in his project and looking forward to the morning. He has "done something" to confirm his worth. The stalker *might not* have done any more than look, "but you never can tell" (106). Haverstraw dubs himself an "emissary of the moon" (106), of Diana, the goddess of chastity and privacy.

The moonlight imagery connects two other conventional characters. The first is the mysterious Janet Manning, an older "Laura." The twenty-year-old Janet recalls a potential lover she apparently met at the beach, "apparently" because her sections are highly romantic, suggestive of the possibility she might have invented the earlier beach encounter. That possibility is supported by her encounter in the present with the same man in a spruce grove that we suspect is sheer fantasy, produced by the night's enchantment. Whether she even left her room is a moot point. Janet is important, however, as Laura's double through the spruce-grove association.

The other associated character is Danny, sketchily developed, perhaps because he is inexperienced like Laura. At the outset Danny is a follower of the "gang-leader," Smitty, who has arrogated to himself this leadership role, based on his experience as a "man." He revels in describing an alleged sexual adventure with a girl for the titillation of Blake and Danny, neither of whom apparently has dated. Blake eggs him on, while Danny says nothing.

The sixteen-year-old Danny is the "nice boy next door," who "has never kissed a girl, never touched a girl" (55). He is a potential "juvenile delinquent," that '50s buzzword, because he is in with "bad company." To prove his manhood by gaining the assertive Smitty's approval, Danny joins Blake as Smitty's accomplice in the library break-in. Like the "girl gang," Smitty's "gang" is bent on simply being where they are not supposed to be. Unlike Blake, however, Danny has the strength to just walk away, in part because he is offended by Smitty's locker-room braggadocio. The night-out exhausts Danny, who falls asleep in his backyard and has a dream encounter with the moon-goddess, as does Laura. He awakes reassured that in his future he will work out this dating challenge successfully, and undoubtedly not in Smitty's manner. Perhaps he might even date Laura. Millhauser wisely resists the impulse to open that door too wide by having Danny, rather than Haverstraw, serve as Laura's rescuer.

In these ways, *Enchanted Night* offers a celebration of a moonlit summer night. The characters are not fully enough developed to transcend two-dimensionality, mainly because Millhauser's emphasis is elsewhere. This "elsewhere" includes, for example, a half-dozen instances of a "Chorus of Night Voices," reminding us that this novella is not simply a narrative of plot and characters. And yet that is what we usually focus on. It is enough for the central characters to have their episodes associated with the night-world, and end with some resolution, or at least something to look forward to the next morning. Millhauser seems to be making an effort to avoid the pronounced ending of "In the Penny Arcade," where the boy undergoes a dramatic change; here, the characters change, but it could be as temporary as the moonlight. The "protagonist," however, is the moon personified as Diana, the huntress-goddess of the moon, womanhood, and privacy/chastity. Diana entices overheated people, even mannequins, out into the night, her realm, where she both exposes and protects vulnerable human beings.

CHAPTER 11

The King in the Tree

The combination of the three novellas in *The King in the Tree* is likely to pique the reader's curiosity, just as the organization of short stories in a collection such as *In the Penny Arcade* raises questions of how the stories fit together. Reviewers generally agreed the three novellas were dark renditions of love relations. Jeff Zaleski writes of "these stories as smart and fresh as they are grim," and Christopher Paddock comments on these "three brilliant novellas" as "each a variation on the theme of heartache: these are tales of love lost, betrayed, or unrequited." In her Sunday *New York Times* review, Laura Miller calls the first of the novellas, "Revenge," a "gothic masterpiece" in focusing on Millhauser's fascination with the "tiger" of the imagination: "This writer is in love with a large, very beautiful and not especially tame tiger, and at its best the fiction he produces is an exquisite negotiation with the beast."[1]

"Revenge" is unquestionably the most dramatic of this triad. The story's premise is that the widow-persona is giving a prospective buyer (and readers who are "listening in") a tour of the house she is selling. An analog is the dramatic monologue as practiced by nineteenth-century English poet Robert Browning. In fact the widower-persona of Browning's famous poem "My Last Duchess" also acts as a house guide and voices resentment against a dead spouse. This widow discloses that her deceased history-professor husband was having an affair and indicates that the prospective buyer was the guilty party.

Readers are drawn into this "whodunit" by the expectation of discovering the full "story." How will the prospective buyer respond to the widow's having fingered her as the "other woman"? How did the hypotenuse of the love triangle go missing? Where is this story leading? Because the widow occasionally speaks with barely contained rage toward her dead husband and more subtly toward the other woman, readers wonder if the story will end with an attempt to harm the widow's listener, who has appeared under false pretenses, as an "innocent" house-hunter, rather than as the "home-wrecker" she is.

Millhauser adapts the focus on architecture evident elsewhere in his fiction to emphasize the implications of individual spaces in a house. From the "Front Hall," opening on the house's public section, with the "Living Room" the widow moves to the "Kitchen," but not without pointing out: "Door to the cellar. Back porch." She announces she wants to show the woman the porch but not the cellar, leading the detective-reader to wonder what may be down there—especially since the widow does not use the contemporary term, "basement," but the old-fashioned term, "cellar."

In the kitchen, traditionally a domestic, "feminine" space, the "heart" of the home, the persona offers the other woman tea and reveals her dead husband's confession of his affair. After allowing her guest to process this revelation and the suspense to build, the persona reveals what some readers suspected: Robert confesses the other woman's name. "Revenge" has begun to take its course as the widow hits her victimizer-victim with an even bigger blow: Robert betrayed his mistress by revealing that she meant nothing to him; she was "just a body" (*The King in the Tree* 13), as though the phrase were Robert's. Perhaps he said that to protect his betrayed wife's feelings; perhaps he was just another husband having a cheap affair. But the tour must move on to the "Back Porch," where there is "so much more to tell" (13), and this "black widow" has a powerful tale to spin for this "fly" she has invited into her "parlor."

In the "Back Porch" section, the widow's tale turns perverse, hinting at her murderous thoughts, following Robert's confession. Intent on poisoning the well of her potential victim's love of Robert, the persona voices the nightmare of any "other woman" by relating the story of entering her rival's home at night and standing over her with a kitchen knife. To turn the knife figuratively, the persona asks if Robert ever shared the story of this and subsequent night visits to demonstrate how little he cared for the other woman, putting her life at risk to continue enjoying her body.

If readers are not totally drawn into the widow's murderous rage, they might begin to sense the claustrophobic, even solipsistic world of the persona's storytelling. With the death of Robert, the widow has absolute control over the narrative; the listener, like the story's readers, has no way to dispute the widow's story of invading the other woman's home and standing over her with a knife. We bandy around the term "insane jealousy," but the power of the persona's revenge plot is so seductive that we believe the storyteller, even though we strongly sense that the story *itself* is the widow's vengeance, and not just its prelude. For example, before going upstairs, the widow shows the other woman the "Dining Room," primarily to tell the story of making love with Robert on his grandmother's table, which she gouged with a knife after his confession.

Of the rooms upstairs, the obviously most important one is the "Bedroom." After cleverly noticing the other woman's hesitancy, the widow invites the woman to lie on the bed with her for some "pillow talk," beginning with the disclosure that it was here she got the call concerning Robert's automobile accident. Slowly, in a whisper, she reveals she knew the other woman violated the sanctity of the marriage bed by moving the adulterous affair there when the widow was visiting her mother. The widow's earlier revelation that early in the marriage Robert was so upset by a spell of impotence he wanted to commit suicide, together with her disclosure of wanting her "murderer" dead, suggests she deliberately precipitated the "accident." A quick trip up to the "Attic" has the sole purpose of reinforcing the suicide notion by showing the other woman where the betrayed wife allegedly made her own attempt.

When the tour moves down to the "Cellar," readers anticipate the persona may be about to actually use a knife this time on her other "murderer." She certainly runs on about cellars being great places to murder and then hack up the body, and how hatred spurred her to do just that. However, she was saved from such mayhem by her imagination allowing her to see the other woman as human and capable of suffering because she too had been in love with Robert and thus was also *vulnerable.* Like the black-widow spider, the persona has been waiting in her "parlor," offering her prey an "open house" tour of her widow's heart. Touring the home she had violated, the other woman could enjoy sympathizing with the woman she "killed" or savor the thrill of triumph, even the *frisson* of guilt in violating this home once again. Now the other woman's only option is to join Robert in committing suicide.[2]

The key element is viewpoint. Told in the first person, the story can also be read as the unnamed widow's fantasy of how she would like to give the other woman a tour of the home she wrecked as a prelude to encouraging her to choose her own method of suicide. Yes, the story is extreme to most readers—except for the thousands of betrayed wives who have survived the violations of their marriages but are secretly attracted to the fantasy of playing Black Widow to the other woman's fly.

The premise of "An Adventure of Don Juan" is that at thirty the legendary "lover," or womanizer, was "hot-blooded and handsome," but tired of his life. After a year, Venice has become a brothel with women throwing themselves at the sexual superstar. Although he has swum the Ebro and "ravished a handsome washerwoman," only to swim back "to complete the seduction of a countess" (57), it was just too easy. Readers may note the classism in his notions of "amorous" couplings: the countess must be seduced, while the washerwoman can be "ravished," or raped, and possibly impregnated to "improve the breed." Indeed the Don relishes the legend that one Venetian street is packed with the mothers of his children. Because Don Juan is the viewpoint character, the narrative reveals the great lover's perception that he "didn't know whether he loved women, but he knew that he loved the pursuit and conquest of women" (58). The narrator, however, can also be critical of Don Juan as one of those "men who prey on women" (62).

Having escaped capture by the husband of his last "conquest" by jumping out the window into the canal, Juan meets the English landowner Augustus Hood, standing in a gondola looking at the stars through a telescope. Hood's invitation to visit Swan Park in Somerset tempts Juan to seek a change of scenery. He accepts Hood's invitation in part because of the eroticized geography of Europe, dividing a sexually open South from a sexually repressed North, promising more challenge from resistant English women to whet his appetite for conquest. Once at Swan Park, Juan sets his sights on Hood's wife Mary and her sister Georgiana. Juan *might* feel some compunction at targeting his host's wife, but would undoubtedly lay the blame at Hood's doorstep for his reclusive lifestyle, which reduced the guest list to Juan.

Juan quickly demonstrates the secret of his success with women: he is a genius at discovering the "slight, subterranean ripples of inclination and repulsion that constituted the hidden life of women" (72). Focusing on Mary who is more responsive—Georgiana keeps her distance—Juan observes that "her interest in him quickened whenever he turned his attention toward Georgiana" (72). It was not yet "jealousy" but a kind of "ownership" that would transform itself into the former. Alone in the park with Mary, Juan tells her she has been avoiding him; her self-defense so clearly demonstrates she loves him that "he was about to seize her and throw her down on the grass" (81), when his host pops out of a hollow tree to show them a flight of stairs to "a splendid system of subterranean tunnels" (82). Hood's interest in architecture and landscaping marks him as a citizen of Millhauser's world.

Juan and the two women becomes a triangle of dissatisfaction. He pursues Georgiana, because he enjoys her resistance, while rejecting Mary who genuinely loves him, because she is a too easy conquest, preferring to think of her as a sister, not a potential lover. Georgiana, in turn, comes to his room and confuses Juan by asking him to be "particularly kind" to her sister. Mary is not eating, growing thin, refusing to see a doctor, and Georgiana knows her sister is "fond" of him. Juan ponders whether Georgiana is being unusually sympathetic to his suffering by encouraging him to make love to Mary as a surrogate. He also tries to imagine that Georgiana is leading him on, pretending to resist his overtures only to mask a "secret passion" (120).

The plot appears to be moving toward its climax when the sleepless Don sees the sleepless Mary approaching and then joining him in bed. The observation that he "crossed his legs irritably" implies what readers have suspected: A sexual athlete has apparently become as celibate as a monk for the weeks since he jumped into a Venetian canal. Poor Juan is aroused by the succubus of Georgiana, while he feels only "an irritable, exasperated tenderness for poor Mary Hood, his pale sister in sorrow" (122). What a predicament for a Don Juan! Three times during the night he turns to Mary, but each time he cannot follow his logic that a woman is a woman, or even make love with her as an act of compassion. Millhauser appears to be exposing the Don as a man who loves women and sexual intimacy far less than the anticipation of gratification, accentuated by his own imagination and the woman's performance of resistance to his charms. Before dawn he wakes the "untouched" Mary so that her husband will not think the worst of her for being in his guest's room.

The next day when Juan rides alone into the country he encounters a shepherd of thirteen or fourteen and a shepherd girl who play at love to mock his aroused gaze before moving off to make love. Humiliated that he, the great lover, has become an object of ridicule, Juan returns to Swan Park, determined to have Georgiana, even by force, if necessary. That night as he wanders looking for Georgiana's room, he encounters the ghost-like Mary, who leaves him, knowing he is pursuing her sister. He finds Georgiana in bed—but not alone, for lying next to her is Augustus Hood to whom he announces his departure the next morning. Despite hearing Mary attempted to drown herself, leaving a note—"HERE LIES MARY HOOD, WHO DIED FOR LOVE"—Juan departs for Venice, where the conquistador belongs, in a world Shakespeare peopled with "the lunatic, the lover, and the poet, who are of imagination all compact."

"The King in the Tree" has its roots in the famous love triangle of King Mark of Cornwall, who sent his nephew Tristan to escort his young bride Ysolt/Iseult/Isolde to his marriage bed, only to discover that his young Queen and his nephew had apparently become lovers. Millhauser used all the available versions of the story but borrowed the name of the French poet Thomas of Britain,[3] whom he makes the narrator/"author" of the novella. This narrative is further shaped by Millhauser's decision to construct an ambivalent position for Thomas. He is an insider, whose loyalty is clearly to the King he serves as a "faithful counselor," but also an outsider, who can only observe and record what he sees and hears, but not penetrate the psyche of the King, the Queen, or Tristan. To further complicate the narrative, Millhauser constricts Thomas's function by establishing this tale as journal entries Thomas "jots down," usually at bedtime. Unlike conventional narrative in which the storyteller has the clear sense of an ending before the first word is said/written because the story's action has been completed, Thomas is telling a story in which he joins his audience in not knowing how it will end, in marked contrast to Jeffrey Cartwright, who knows everything that has happened when he begins to tell his story.

Essentially the love triangle is a combination of figures with wide appeal to the medieval European imagination. The King has married a beautiful young woman, whose feeling for him is "married love," while she in turn has been attracted to a handsome younger man for whom she feels a variety of "romantic love," made the more intense and powerful because it is socially forbidden. Additionally because she is Queen such love is also politically taboo. In betraying the King, she and her lover have committed treason, given that the King is the State.

Because the storyteller Thomas is the King's councilor, he is privy to what is said at court when the King is not present. Hearing rumors about the Queen and Tristan, Thomas concludes: "They are too much together" (145). And he is intimately aware of Court intrigue. The King's steward Oswin,[4] for example, resents the Queen and Tristan's power. Were they eliminated, he would be the King's favorite and better able to abscond with royal possessions he is rumored to be looting. Oswin finds an ally in the leading Court dwarf Modor, whose physical deformity mirrors his ugly soul. Eventually the two will conspire to uncover the Queen and Tristan's affair through a "dumb show," reminiscent of *Hamlet,* in which Modor and a female dwarf impersonate the lovers. And even the Queen's handmaid Bragane has a role in the intrigue as a messenger and agent for her mistress's interests.

The position Thomas has been forced into is extremely complicated. Uppermost in the councilor's priorities is the King he serves. Thomas dislikes the Queen and though he loves Tristan, that love is less than what he feels for his King. Thomas is exquisitely sensitive to the King's impossible dilemma. The two people he loves most in the world appear to be in love with each other. The Queen came to him as the realization of that woman who haunts men's dreams: young, beautiful, and presumably innocent. The narrative as controlled by Thomas eliminates the possibility of the Wagnerian rendition in which on shipboard Tristan and Isolde drink what they later learn was a love potion, served to them by Isolde's handmaid Bragane, and the bride enters Mark's bed as no longer a maiden. The King's love for Tristan is a father's love for a son, who will become the next king if the marriage bed proves unfruitful—as it seems to have in Millhauser's version, even though much is made of the love-making in the Royal Bedchamber, and Tristan and Ysolt may have regularly made love too.

The story's action is generated by the King's effort to believe in the fidelity of his nephew and his wife, on the one hand, and his own occasional lapses of faith in them, on the other. To scotch rumors about his wife and nephew, he insists that Tristan serve as the Queen's protector throughout the day, only further feeding the rumor mill. When he decides to entrap the Queen and Tristan by watching them from a tree—thus the novella's title—and when he later sends Tristan away, he feels he has betrayed both his wife and nephew by not trusting their fidelity. Furthermore the King may sense that Tristan and the Queen pose the ultimate challenge to his love for both, for the highest expression of love may be to desire what the loved one most desires. Ideally the loved one will *not* want another, but what if she or he does? The sticking point is the King's position: Mark knows that to his subjects a king who cannot maintain his own wife's loyalty is unlikely to preserve his subjects' allegiance.

Because the storyteller Thomas's deepest affection is for the King, the focus is the incredible suffering of a noble heart, torn between the desire to remain faithful to those he loves and the increasing evidence that those he loves are bound by a "higher love" for each other. Other renditions of the story such as Wagner's *Tristan and Isolde* invest in the tragedy of the lovers by making them the centerpiece. Millhauser chooses to invest in them indirectly, as their story is filtered through his narrator Thomas, for whom the focus is the suffering King in a double bind. Thus, when rumors arrive that Tristan has married another Ysolt and Thomas is sent to verify the rumors, the narrator himself becomes part of the plot.

It is Thomas's visit that seals the fate of first Tristan and then Ysolt. When the two men are alone, Tristan demands, "Tell me she no longer loves me!" Thomas writes ambivalently, "I gave him the assurance he sought," presumably that Ysolt continues to love him. However, this assertion of her fidelity follows the revelation of the narrator's fateful thought: "[I]s it perhaps the solution? Tristan dead, Tristan out of it?" This willingness to think about a form of euthanasia for Tristan may be a justification for the stress Thomas lays on Tristan's tragic ending as a necessity, even a mercy because he cannot stop loving Ysolt, nor she him. Thus Thomas includes what his servant heard from one of Tristan's men, that is, that Tristan has refused to consummate his marriage to the child-bride who lies beside him each night with open eyes.

The stage is set for a tragic climax when the wounded Tristan's life hangs in the balance, as he wonders whether his lover Ysolt will come to save him as she did in Ireland when he came for her. If she is on the arriving ship, it is to show a white sail; if not, a black. Tristan's wife shouts down from her window that the sail is black, and Thomas hesitates to contradict her, even though he knows it is white and the false report will rob Tristan of the will to live.[5] When the Queen arrives, she throws herself on Tristan's corpse, never to rise again, and Thomas will have served his suffering master, whom he hopes will now be able to go forward. Perhaps Thomas will succeed in saving his King, perhaps this world has no place for the Tristans and Ysolts, perhaps intense, passionate love must either modulate into "married love" or perish. In any case this Celtic tale with Irish versions in which the names are King Conchubar and the lovers are Deirdre and Naoise, and Cornish versions in which King Arthur, Queen Guinevere, and Lancelot fill out the roles continued in modern times in W. B. Yeats's play *Deirdre of the Sorrows* and the musical *Camelot,* respectively.

Given that Millhauser himself grouped these three novellas together, readers are impelled to consider their interrelationships. The three tales share concerns with love between women and men in triangular constructions. In the first, Millhauser offers a powerfully chilling view of how the suffering of a woman betrayed by her husband and the other woman can produce an obsession with vengeance. In the second, Millhauser borrows the Don Juan figure to explore a paradox of love: Juan rejects the woman who loves him so completely she literally cannot live without him, while he pursues her "sister," whose rejection whets his appetite. The story's climax is a joke on Juan the great lover, who never figures out that he may be rejected by the sister he pursues because she has captured the love of her brother-in-law, whose wife may know of the affair and pursue Juan the more. The dark melodrama of the first novella and the somber comedy of the second give way to the tragedy of the third. Here not only the figures are part of the reader's ken, but the story's ending is fixed, giving Millhauser's tale a sense of fate, which cannot be altered. Central is the King, who if he had been the narrator of the first novella would have had the lovers slain in short order for treason. Instead, his is a long-suffering love that *almost* qualifies him for sainthood—"almost" because a saint of Love would have certified Tristan as Crown Prince and then walked into the sea. But then like passionate lovers such as Tristan and Ysolt, saints are useful as ideals, but have no viable place among us mere mortals.

CHAPTER 12

Dangerous Laughter: Thirteen Stories

Readers may be surprised to begin *Dangerous Laughter* (2008) with "Cat 'n' Mouse," under the rubric "Opening Cartoon." Some may wonder: If the first selection is the "*Opening* Cartoon," will the stories to follow also be "cartoons"? Is Millhauser himself playing "cat 'n' mouse" with his readers by beginning with a cartoon? And in the end will we "cats" find out what kind of game this shrewd "mouse" is playing? Since cartoons such as "Tom and Jerry" end in a stalemate in the conflict, will the author withhold an ending and forego the traditional power of transmitting "meaning," choosing instead to offer a narrative that merely "stops"?

A story that stops, not ends, is a distinct possibility, given the ambiguity of the term "cartoon." When we speak, for example, of a "Tom and Jerry" cartoon, we refer to one short, animated film, but also to the seemingly endless series of episodes in which a cat obsessively pursues a clever mouse, which inevitably escapes. Not only does the cartoon generate slapstick comedy through the cat's ludicrous machinations; it also offers comedy in the audience's foreknowledge that the mouse *must* escape or there could be no "sequel." Accordingly the endless pursuit of the cat's "game," or "prey," is as obsessive as the narrative form representing the game.

To explore the cartoon form, the author takes readers into the thoughts of both antagonists to understand why a cartoon series can go on forever. The cat is aware his obsessive pursuit will inevitably fail, but he cannot stop because what else would he do? Similarly the mouse knows he will always succeed but risks the boredom that could jeopardize his future. Furthermore, although he would like a shrewder opponent to provide more challenge, he realizes it could bring on the unthinkable.

In the end "Cat 'n' Mouse" is a story about itself, a story about storytelling. The author unmasks himself, revealing his awareness that he is playing the game of "art" with us "cats," who want to know where this story is going. As the storytelling mouse knows full well, we cats obsessively pursue a story's ending to grasp its meaning because it boosts our faith that Life has meaning. Thus the author/narrator offers us an "ending."

Like the "final episode" in a television series, "Cat 'n' Mouse" attempts to transcend mere stopping by ending with a final cartoon. Millhauser's mouse succeeds by methodically eradicating the pursuing cat, literally erasing him with a red handkerchief, then the cartoon's scenery, and finally himself. Putting the story under erasure leaves only the red handkerchief, which transforms itself into theater curtains, across which "words write themselves in black script: THE END" (*Dangerous Laughter* 18). We cats have our desire satisfied, but this wish-fulfillment is also a self-erasure: the contagion of the story's ending, or death, wipes out its readers by rendering them functionless. That is how we smart cats learn the painful paradox of reading: we both want and do not want to know how it ends because ending erases the reading experience, as well as the reader.[1]

In "Contents" readers discover the map of *Dangerous Laughter,* or more precisely the "blueprint" of its "architecture." The twelve stories that follow "Cat 'n' Mouse" are organized in three groups of four, making "Cat 'n' Mouse" a "pinnacle," leading readers down to the building itself. Each foursome has its own title, marking it off as a separate architectural unit within the larger structure.

The first story in "Vanishing Acts"—"The Disappearance of Elaine Coleman"—seems a straightforward missing-person case. This haunting story draws upon the mystery or detective-story form: Elaine has "gone missing," and the first-person-plural narrator[2] becomes a detective assembling clues to solve the mystery of her disappearance. Additionally the story resembles a magic trick of how this female Houdini escaped her room, with the only viable exit locked from the inside. In the narrator's scrupulously searching his memory of his classmate and finding little "evidence," the narrative is encouraging readers to suspect this may be an unsolvable case. The case both is and is not solved when the narrator concludes that Elaine evaporated into thin air, a phrase the narrative is de-familiarizing. "The Lady Vanishes" here because the community—and the *narrator*—carelessly neglected to "give her the time of day." Obviously Millhauser is not "preaching" about our casual cruelty in not so much shunning but simply ignoring "singles," thereby modeling in the narrator the feeling of suddenly becoming aware of the impact our lack of concern can have on someone who "lives alone."

Although not identified as a novella, "The Room in the Attic" gives the impression of one through an extended time-span—roughly a half-year—and its more complex development. The narrative returns to Millhauser's earlier interest in young-adult life in *Portrait of a Romantic.* The sheer boredom of high school in small-town America once again spontaneously generates hunger for excitement, intensity, passion in the narrator, David, a "good boy," with a "good home," straight As, and a "semiofficial girlfriend."

"Wolf," or John Wolfson, is everything Dave secretly wants to be—independent-spirited, lackadaisical, affluent, good-looking enough to rate girls' smiles. Wolf's sister, Isabel, is many times more unconventional than he—so shy that she refuses to meet Dave except in her completely darkened room. As Dave continues to visit Isabel's room, Wolf gradually fades from his consciousness as a fixture of the day-world, while Dave is deeply attracted to Isabel's darkened room as a replication of the night-world he prefers. Neither she nor he wants to let in light, but eventually the darkness speaks to Dave's passionate desire to preserve the "magic of the night," offering another example of Millhauser's attraction to the night-world.[3]

When Isabel decides to "come out" into the light and the day-world's activities, Dave undergoes a panic attack as she starts to pull down the heavy, dusty window-drapes. He seems even more distraught than Arthur Grumm, confronting Eleanor Schumann's similar return to the day-world. Dave desperately covers his eyes to protect them from the "brilliant light outside, raised like a sword" (72). He turns his back on Isabel at the bare window, but "through [his] fingers [he] could feel the room filling with light as if a fire had broken out" (73), and he frantically runs from Isabel's self-exposure. This chapter is entitled "Revelation" because the narrative reveals to readers, if not to Dave, that he has become obsessed with darkness as a refusal to say "yes" to light, and life itself.

As September and Dave's senior year approach, Wolf and Isabel suddenly vanish. Their mother reports that Wolf will spend his last year at a Massachusetts boarding school and Isabel will live with her aunt in Maine, where she will finish high school. Dave returns to the semiofficial girlfriend, and so forth, and readers suspect the narrative represents a rite of passage. Facing his last year of childhood, Dave has invested himself imaginatively in the Wolfsons to cope with approaching adulthood. The abruptness of Wolf's arrival and his gradual fading as Dave enters Isabel's night-world may lead readers to suspect that Isabel's self-confinement to her darkened sanctuary is a radically more dramatic version of Wolf's retreat from the tedium of high school in the day-world. There is a nice ambivalence in the ending: Dave returns to "normal" life, but he does so with a sense of irrevocable loss of the night-world as imagination's matrix.

As in the preceding story and partially in "Room," "Dangerous Laughter" returns to familiar Millhauser territory—adolescence in small-town America a half-century ago, most fully realized in *Portrait of a Romantic.* Also familiar is the first-person-plural narration. As in "The Disappearance of Elaine Coleman," the "we" shifts to an "I," in this case an "I" who is an unnamed, adolescent male narrator/spokesman for the group, bursting with unfulfilled desire for intensity and passion, and bored silly longing for *something* to do while waiting for the future to arrive. Today, that "something" might be alcohol, marijuana, glue-sniffing, Ecstasy, or good old sex. Sexual activity in Millhauser's adolescent world is the province of those other than the stories' central characters. In this more innocent world, the "something" teenagers find to stave off boredom is laughter competitions, which "go viral."

The course of this "rage" itself is conventional. Initially laughter is spontaneously generated by repeating an ordinary word—"cheese"—until it becomes hilarious. The next stage involves "laugh parties," participants competing to laugh harder and longer. Parties give way to "laugh clubs," for which Bernice Alderson is credited, "or laugh parlors, as they were sometimes called" (77), modeled perhaps on "massage parlors." Here laughers strip, get chained to beds, and tickled until they are delirious. Then rumors spread that secret tickling games occur, resembling sexual molestation: a mother catches her nineteen-year-old tickling his seven-year-old sister until she shrieks uncontrollably. The narrator's addiction becomes so complete that the hours between laughter "fixes" become sheer agony.

This communal addiction to laughter becomes more "dangerous," if not perverse. The focus becomes Clara Schuler, a "sister" to Elaine Coleman—a quiet, unassuming, "good girl." This focus makes her a prime candidate for laughter addiction when her "one friend" Helen Jacoby brings her along to a laughter party. Quickly Clara becomes the "life of the party," underlining how the more self-repressed the neophyte the more likely severe addiction will become. Eventually Clara "o.d.s" on laughter, although the death certificate claims she died of a "ruptured blood vessel in her brain" (91). This "tragedy" accelerates a craze of weeping, in which Clara did not participate and from which the "I" narrator distances himself. "Weeping parties" flourish and quickly dissipate, perhaps because laughter has no gender, while weeping is still gendered "feminine." Looking up at Clara's window, the narrator, for example, finds himself laughing, perhaps a reminder that this "I" disapproved of her taking laughter to an extreme but also celebrated it. The closing sentence—"Tomorrow something was bound to happen" (93)—suggests there is no "cure" for adolescent boredom, except adulthood and accepting boredom as "life."

Readers are likely to note how increasingly metaphorical the "Vanishing Acts" are becoming and how these "disappearances" are announced by the mouse's literal vanishing act in the prologue/opening story. In contrast to characters in the first two stories, Clara "vanishes" into uncontrolled laughter, and then into death. And in this section's last story, "History of a Disturbance," the speaker/narrator "vanishes" into silence.

The word *speaker* is appropriate since this story is an uninterrupted monologue with Elena, the unnamed man's wife, as audience. The speaker's "disturbance" begins with Elena's unsettling him by saying at a picnic for two, "'What a wonderful day!'" (96). Elena further unsettles him with her question at the Polinzanos' barbecue: "'Do you love me?'" (98). This incident raises the stakes for the speaker, who cannot decide which of the many possible meanings the question's asker meant him to respond to as well as which of the many possible responses the questioner expected. Readers also become "unsettled" at recognizing how claustrophobic they feel within the small room of the narration, absolutely controlled by a speaker who begins to sound "disturbed" in interrogating language as communication, extensively and rather lyrically but also disturbingly.

That impression is radically accentuated when he reports the next event in this "history." This time it is the supermarket checkout girl saying, "'Have a good day.'" She stuns him with an exclamation whose meaning completely mystifies him, even though his earlier teasing out of "'Do you love me?'" implied recognition of language as verbal massage. Eventually the speaker argues at length and with powerfully poetic language that language blocks direct contact with our world. Having lost faith in language's power to communicate, he passes Elena a note to the effect that he has decided to remain silent. Now we know why his monologue began, "'You are angry, Elena'" (95). An excessive concentration on language that began the "dangerous laughter" of that story, here precipitates a "disturbance," one step from psychosis. And ironically the man is "speaking" this story to Elena in gorgeous, lush language, after he has taken a vow of silence and begun communicating only through gestures.

In "Impossible Architectures," "The Dome" is very familiar Millhauser territory. Indeed it might be generalized that architecture is a signature of the author's subject matter and style in his shorter fiction and preeminently in *Martin Dressler.*[4] Furthermore "The Dome" certainly *is* an architectural term.

The story records a history of developing biospheres as environments for those who want the power and privilege of shutting out the elements. As a pseudo-prospectus for the sale of such domes, this "story" without a plot or characters asserts that it is an understatement to say this dome is the "single largest achievement in the history of architecture" (118). Because everything now is "indoors," Nature has been "abolished." By the end the narrator is enthusing about rumors of a colossal project to encase the entire planet in a "transparent globe" so that Earth itself will become entirely "indoors," comfortable, secure, and presumably habitable.

"In the Reign of Harad IV" moves from the science-fiction world of "The Dome" into an alternative, quasi-historical world, reminiscent of novellas such as "The Princess, the Dwarf, and the Dungeon." "Reign" also returns to Millhauser's fascination with miniatures, evident as early as "Cathay." In Harad IV's kingdom, the maker of miniatures is held in high regard: he has an apartment in the palace, an ermine robe to wear during Court ceremonies, and two young assistants. Like Millhauser's earlier artists/craftsmen, this unnamed miniaturist is driven to further refinements of his work: from a cherry pit he carves a circle of elephants, each holding another's tail in its trunk. When the king lifts a thimble he finds a replica of his toy palace's wing. Unsatisfied with his accomplishments, this artist pushes on to create an absolutely "impossible architecture"—a miniature of the palace, visible only with a magnifying glass. Working alone, he becomes lonely, and even the visit of two apprentices offers no solace. They take turns viewing and lauding the invisible palace, but the miniaturist claims they saw nothing of what he sees. Readers suspect the miniaturist's work is "invisible" because the artist has moved into a solipsistic world of his own in which he sees what he desperately needs to see, reminiscent of Franklin Payne's crossing over into his fantasy world.

"The Other Town" demonstrates a range of credibility in this section's four stories. Unlike the other three, with their serious challenges to the reader's belief in encasing our planet in a biosphere, or building a tower so high no one in a lifetime can climb higher than its lowest levels, "The Other Town" is much more "grounded" in a world like ours, as seen through the eyes of a highly imaginative author.

This story benefits from Millhauser's penchant for first-person-plural point of view. The spokesman explains the patently bizarre maintenance of an absolute replica of their town, not to inhabit but to visit. If all four stories in "Impossible Architectures" are varieties of speculative fiction, "Other Town" seems more believable because the narrator draws readers in with the proposition that a community would maintain its "other" to serve the desire for "presence" through the other's being empty. Since our town never visits the other town en masse, a single visitor might perceive its emptiness, then return home with a renewed sense of our town's plenitude.

Believability in this "other town" is further enhanced by embedding the replica in history. The other town's first recorded history was in 1685, four decades after the original town was settled, thereby locating both in the earliest European settlement of America. Because "the other town" has existed for roughly three centuries, the replica is no recent hare-brained concept but a traditional construct, maintained by many generations.

Another factor affecting believability is the reader's recognition of a perhaps embarrassing curiosity about the interiors of others' homes. That impulse to explore the private spaces of neighbors' homes is legendary in real estate sales in which curious neighbors will pose as prospective buyers to "inspect" others' homes. Thus privacy begets a compulsion to see what is behind others' closed doors.

One other factor is replication—the hourly changes wrought by the "replicators" in this "other town" to match daily changes in "our town." Thus a visitor can keep updated on changes in other residents' homes and admire the craft of replicators in spotting changes in the visitor's home. It *is* a two-edged sword, however, because these "replicators" have an incredibly intrusive presence in our homes as the price of gratifying our curiosity about each other's inner sanctums. In the end the narrator underestimates the efficacy and cost of maintaining this "other town" as a museum[5] as well as the willingness of anyone to sacrifice privacy for any benefits the other town might offer.

"The Other Town" leaves the narrator positioned between the two towns. He asks provocative questions such as: "Exactly where I am, when I stand there and look both ways, who can say?" But his question about this third in-between place, or perhaps *no* place, implies the associated questions: Who am I when I am poised between two worlds? And what does it feel like to be between the everyday world and its "invented" mirror-image?

The "impossible architecture" offered by the next story, "The Tower," is a rendition of a "mythical" past. It is the author's intent to rework the Genesis story of the Tower of Babel, as hinted at in the "Shinar" allusion.[6] As Millhauser has indicated, he sought to build his tower to actually reach heaven before it begins to show signs of collapse. In Genesis a people speaking the same language migrated from the east to the Plain of Shinar, there to build a tower to heaven to establish themselves as one people. Appalled by this hubris, Jehovah decided to confound their single language into many and scatter them around the world, a myth explaining our polyglot world.

Although the Tower of Babel was never finished, Millhauser's Tower is allowed to reach "heaven" as a testimony to human overreaching. "The Tower" appeals to the human impulse to look upward and outward from Earth to "the heavens," patently evident in "ad astra, per aspera," "Heaven above," and in the costly exploration of space. As Millhauser's tower soars, its residents become aware that no individual can hope to achieve the tower's top in a lifetime. Recognizing this, the tower's residents adopt a generational strategy in the hope that great-great-grandchildren might complete the family journey.

Setting aside the feasibility of family journeys, the narrative is more concerned with those living in this "Tower," as a metaphor for our "gendering." The farther up residents live, the more they learn from those descending the tower and the more they aspire to climb higher. Likewise, the lower the residents live, the more they maintain connections with earthly concerns, primarily keeping the species alive. As in "The Other Town," where occasionally residents stop between the twin communities and sense an invisible, third "community" in between, this narrative focuses on our complexly gendered being as a dynamic struggle of "feminine" and "masculine" impulses, neither of which is superior or inferior, both being necessary to remain fully human. All of this speculation is rendered moot by the end, however, when the tower moves toward collapse.

"Here at the Historical Society," the first story in the "Heretical Histories" section, demonstrates the continuing attraction of first-person-plural point of view to Millhauser. The unnamed narrator/speaker is delivering what becomes an increasingly hostile defense of a new definition of local history. Emphasizing the Historical Society's "tireless pursuit of the past" (161), or more specifically how much unpaid overtime its members contribute to the community, the speaker asserts how "wildly irresponsible" it is to criticize the society for "recent changes" as representing a lack of "love for the past" (161–62). As the speaker's voice becomes shriller and more defensive, readers wonder about the legitimacy of this criticism.

Having detailed the society's commitment to the "Old Past," the speaker describes the "New Past," which has generated the community's criticism. The society now operates on the principle that "the present is *the past made visible*" (165). Through exhibits of litter (Popsicle wrappers, cigarette packages, and so forth), or a film of a backyard with an eight-hour running time, or audiotapes of conversation in a local supermarket, the society asks visitors to credit seeming trivia with the status of the contents of King Tut's tomb. Apparently supermarket chatter is as valid a historical artifact as the lost plays of Sophocles. In closing, the speaker asks critics essentially to recognize a leveling of values so everything is equally deserving of preservation, since the present can never accurately foresee what the future will value: "For once you accept the New Past, nothing is unworthy of your closest and most reverent attention" (169).

At the same time, the reader ought not to discard the principles of the "New Past," with which the Historical Society began, since those principles have a resonance in contemporary thought. Many have accepted the notion that "history" is not restricted to the lives of the rich and powerful, along with the wars they have fought to gain or protect their wealth and power. Increasingly we have focused, for example, not only on the role of the political leaders and generals in the "War Between the States" but also on the parts played by women and slaves. As in much of Millhauser's other fiction, we see something valuable pushed to an extreme, whether Dressler's hotel innovations or Sarabee's amusement-park improvements. This impulse to innovate, to go the next step, to push against the limits is the human tendency to overreach, which can end in tragedy, or something resembling satire, which exaggerates to return us to moderation.

"A Change of Fashion," the next "heretical history," is likely to surprise readers who might not expect Millhauser to write a satirical piece on the power of fashion designers and the silliness of changing fashions in women's apparel. Appearing first in *Harper's,* this story was reprinted in the women's magazine *Elle.* The author has clearly done his research to "talk" like a fashion designer of "crimson silk half-slips with side slits, stretch satin and dotted-mesh chemises with ruffle trim" (174).[7] Further analysis, however, reveals the author following a frequent pattern of a notion or creation developed further and further until it implodes, as in "Paradise Park" and *Martin Dressler.*

In its own way "A Precursor of the Cinema" is also bizarre. The narrative is anything but unusual in its focus on the forerunners of film in the later nineteenth century. "Eisenheim the Illusionist" has hints of Millhauser's research in that area, especially the connections between illusionism, or staged magic, and early film, which drew in crowds for showings of very brief, filmed documentaries of the most prosaic, everyday events. Other earlier Millhauser fiction also offers evidence of his interest in film, and animation generally. "Franklin Payne" is a brilliant portrait of a "pioneer" of animated film who devotes himself so completely that his daughter is his sole meaningful contact with the world. And "August Eschenburg" is yet another artist of animation, who dedicates himself to the presumably impossible task of creating the successful replication of the human body's movement. And there is also "The New Automaton Theater" with its complex exploration of illusionism and the pursuit of verisimilitude.

In "Precursor," Millhauser performs his own variety of the "Verisimilism" of his artist-figure Harlan Crane. Introduced in the context of the big names of later nineteenth-century inventors and their inventions, ranging from the "false line" of Daguerre's Diorama to the "true line" of "Plateau's Phenakistoscope, Horner's Zoetrope, and Reynaud's Praxinoscope" (179), Crane is provided with such a detailed biographical sketch that Millhauser succeeds in passing him off as such a convincingly "real" precursor of film that readers may find themselves Googling the name to make sure Crane is not an actual artist/inventor. For an author reluctant to reveal details of his own biography, it is ironic that Millhauser musters up such a semblance of a biography that the reader is persuaded Crane was a historical figure.

Crane began as a painter, a Verisimilist, to use Millhauser's term for an ersatz artistic style. Contrary to the conventional notion that later nineteenth-century painting moved toward the Impressionism of Renoir and especially Monet in large part to transcend the competition of the photograph, Verisimilism sought the "verisimilitude," or exactitude of detail made possible by the camera. In his early career, Crane invented minor, mechanically produced expressions of illusionism, such as a doll with a mechanical heartbeat, and more important, his Phantasmatrope. When turned, Crane's Phantasmatrope produced effects similar to the zoetrope with its series of sequential images, which, if spun fast enough, gave the illusion of continuous movement.

The failure of Crane's illusionist inventions impelled him to invent "animate paint." (185).[8] Once Millhauser has grounded his artist figure in premodern production of devices providing the magic of motion, the narrative is prepared to move into the fantasy world in which a chemical compound can animate the object the artist paints. For example, the artist can paint a still life of a fruit bowl with conventional paint as "scenery" for a fly painted with this "animate paint," causing the viewer to be startled by the fly taking off from the fruit and then landing there. In a sense this fantasy narrative is Millhauser's "invention," for if he succeeds in painting Crane's life and works convincingly, readers may find themselves temporarily suspending disbelief in the author's own illusionist endeavor, especially when he brings in the early efforts of the Lumière brothers and Thomas Edison to trick their viewers' eyes into seeing "moving pictures." It is no coincidence that a pioneer in filmmaking, Georges Méliès, began as a stage magician.

Millhauser's work as an illusionist continues in his biography of Crane, whose paintings are varieties of magic acts. The author even offers a reprise of the Moorash exhibition-catalog device to work his magic in describing four "animate" paintings to support the assertion of this story's title, "A Precursor of the Cinema," that is, the work of Edison and the Lumières. Crane's biography continues with his being expelled from the Verisimilist movement, his acceptance within the Transgressive movement, and his finishing several "animate" paintings, complete with further exhibition cataloging.

Soon Millhauser's descriptions recall "The Tale of Ignotus" in *From the Realm of Morpheus,* where the portrait-figure can leave the painting and return. Crane's paintings eventually cause such notoriety that the Transgressive movement breaks up, after viewers fear that a knife could leave the painting and wound them. Crane becomes a recluse, known only through diary entries of fellow Transgressive W. C. Curtis. The "animate" painter becomes a photographer, a stage performer, for which he garners notoriety as a "charlatan" before returning to painting with *Picnic on the Hudson,* a huge animate work, which causes a sensation among viewers. Another work, *Terra Incognita,* causes a greater stir when spectators experience tactile responses caused by shadowy figures that leave the painting, suggesting similar figures in Moorash's later work, the figures Eisenheim calls up, and the haptograph in the next story. Panic ensues, a woman is trampled, the Pantoptic Theater is closed, Crane abandons public life.

This long story continues for several pages, tracing the latter days of a broken man who has essentially outlived his life. But then Crane appears to stage an ambiguous comeback with *Swan Song,* a Verisimilist rendering of his studio, with the painter at work on his signature painting, *Picnic on the Hudson.* In *Swan Song* are representations of all his paintings in a studio, accurate down to a mouse's tail. The latter detail recalls "Cat 'n' Mouse," as Crane's paintings erase themselves, and Crane at his easel fades away, never to be seen again, just as his paintings are never found. The ending recalls "Eisenheim the Illusionist" and that illusionist's apotheosis in making himself disappear, and once again, the boy in the final frames of Franklin Payne with his magic eraser. Paradoxically, by erasing all his work and himself, Harlan has validated the success of his animate painting method as a forerunner of filmmaking.

Millhauser leaves until last one of the collection's most surprisingly provocative stories. Who would think that a story told as journal entries of an unnamed technician in Thomas Edison's New Jersey laboratory could move us with its tragic sense of the lost opportunity to pursue an invention with breathtaking possibilities? The story's title, "The Wizard of West Orange," signals Millhauser's impulse to explore research in that modern sorcerer's workshop where a sorcerer's apprentice, Kistenmacher, has become obsessed with the invention of a haptographic device with the power to transmit tactile sensations to the wearer. The journal-style narrative manages to catch the excitement of the narrator's response to Edison's own obsession with a flood of new inventions, an obsessive pursuit of where the imagination leads some of Edison's staff who have caught the contagion of a wizard too excited to sleep more than a few hours. The Wizard's "eyes are blue fire" (235).

The narrator becomes Kistenmacher's prime subject in his experiments with the haptograph after his colleague Earnshaw asks to be removed from the assignment on moral grounds. Even the narrator displays surprising modesty in taking off his shirt while Kistenmacher turns his back, and when the device becomes a full-body suit Kistenmacher sends the narrator behind a screen to don the haptograph. The narrator becomes enthralled by not only the device's power to transmit familiar tactile sensations but also new ones.

It is the potential for erotic sensation that ultimately dooms the invention once others in the laboratory begin openly joking that the haptograph will eventually eliminate a man's need of a woman. Like the knocking of fate on the door, the destruction of the haptograph prototype occurs when Earnshaw gains access to the "Box" where the experiments are done and tears the device to pieces. Tellingly the Wizard merely fires Earnshaw and quietly shuts down Kistenmacher's work, impelling the narrator to deduce that Edison shared Earnshaw's sentiment that the haptograph's focus on touch and intimacy smack of the apple in Eden. The narrator is not far from the truth in rationalizing the Wizard's abandonment of the haptograph as the Master's obsession with profitability and his often boyish inability to concentrate on an invention such as the movie camera allow his competitors to temporarily outrun him in advancing film technology. At the same time, the Wizard may have retreated from the taboo of touch.

Then again the collection gains measurably in the book-ending of this story and the first, "Cat 'n' Mouse." As the first story grounds itself in animated cartoons, a dominant genre of "popular culture," this last story takes readers into the laboratory of the "Wizard," who made sound technology and film possible. Both stories reveal Millhauser's openness to expressions of modernity that the gurus of "high culture," modernists such as Ezra Pound and T. S. Eliot, could see only as the first waves of a sea of barbarism, threatening to deluge the later twentieth century. Perhaps more than earlier collections of Millhauser's fiction, *Dangerous Laughter* reveals the breadth and depth of the author's fiction.

CHAPTER 13

We Others: New and Selected Stories

We Others: New and Selected Stories (2011) marks a milestone in Steven Millhauser's career. Like *Dangerous Laughter,* this collection was published by Knopf, the publisher of *Edwin Mullhouse,* and long respected for the fiction the press publishes. Additionally the "New and Selected" organization of *We Others* acknowledges that Millhauser has been publishing fiction long enough to be more than due for a "Selected." In his "Author's Note," Millhauser explains his initial effort to choose "representative" stories, but after deciding the stories he omitted were just as representative as those he chose, he abandoned that approach. He opted instead for stories that impressed him as though they were written by someone else.

The first new story, "The Slap," is written from a favorite Millhauser point of view—the first-person-plural—justified by a community, collectively attempting to make sense of a series of bizarre incidents. First Walter Lasher and eventually six others encounter a thirty-something man, who suddenly appears and without warning slaps each in the face so hard that the victim is too startled to respond before the slapper disappears. Eventually, after the slapper strikes several times, "we" focus on the term "victim," generalizing that the slaps might not seem to justify the term: "Even so, it seemed to most of us that the suddenness of the attack, the strength of the slap, the apparent randomness, the anger and helplessness induced in the person receiving the slap" (*We Others* 14) justified the term.

The story invests the most attention in Walter Lasher because his reaction is the most complicated. Readers can understand his being particularly startled not only because he is the first but also because he is tall and powerfully built. Lasher quickly recalls not having been assaulted since Jimmy Kubec shoved him in sixth grade and he then broke Jimmy's nose. Lasher immediately tries to rationalize the episode: The slapper may have mistaken him for someone else; he may be deranged or a client of Lasher's whose portfolio has suffered from the economic downturn. Perhaps Lasher unwittingly offended the slapper. Then he curiously persuades himself it is too late to call the police, but he *will* tell his wife. When he wakes in the night, Lasher immediately recalls breaking Jimmy's nose, suggesting he may be feeling long-delayed guilt for his boyhood violence.

Two mornings after waking from the nose-breaking dream, Lasher reads in the newspaper at breakfast that Robert Sutliff has been slapped. Again his response is curious: he feels relieved he had not been singled out, but no responsibility for Sutliff's assault, even though his failure to report his slap made it possible for the slapper to strike again. Later he considers reporting it only because he thinks Sutliff was a poor observer. But Lasher has not told even his wife, making readers more curious why Lasher is so unsettled by the slap.

That curiosity is fed by continuing attention to Walter Lasher, who practically snubs a female friend in the hardware store and becomes so secretive that his wife prefers he *not* come home from work. The extent of Lasher's psychological injury from being slapped is measured by his misrecognizing Dr. Daniel Ettlinger as the slapper, who might be broadening his modus operandi by attempting a repeat slap. When Lasher slaps Ettlinger to forestall a second episode, both men are arrested. Lasher adds to the community's angst by revealing that he never reported being the first victim.

The community's efforts to explain these slaps continue to be undercut. When Charles Kraus, who is returning from his work in the city, becomes the next victim, some speculate the slapper is targeting affluent commuters from their "bedroom community." The slap of a cable repairman, Raymond Sorenson, undermines that "theory." And then the slapping of the high-school student Sharon Hands broadens the victims by gender, just as the slapping of Valerie Kozlowski in her own home in the evening ratchets up the community's fear by another notch.

The last victim is young newspaper reporter Matthew Dennis, tasked with riding the commuter train from Manhattan and taking note of the passengers' comments. Matthew's theory is that the slapper is reminding his victims of something they did and want to forget. True to form, the trench-coated slapper nails Matthew, immersed in speculation about the slapper's motives. Matthew's article theorizing that the victims are chosen just because they live in this town alienates many of his readers by appearing sympathetic to the slapper.

Although Millhauser's readers expect an explanation, he offers a taste of realism by stopping rather than ending the story. If readers have been "armchair detectives," following the story carefully to figure out "whodunit," and why, "all" they find is an even more unsettling outcome. The slapper merely disappears without a trace, leaving the narrator as well as the story's readers with the enigma of the slapper's motives—not only why he began slapping the townsfolk but why he stopped. Yet another element of indeterminacy is the distinct possibility that he might return to continue his slapping.

Although a "New" story, "Tales of Darkness and the Unknown, Vol. XIV: The White Glove," suggests by its long title that it has been "Selected" from a series of similar stories, comprising at least fourteen volumes. Like "The Slap," "The White Glove" is an expression of Sigmund Freud's "unheimlich," or the "uncanny," the "heimlich" representing the "homely," everyday, or familiar. These two stories unsettle readers by de-familiarizing the ordinariness of, say, walking safely in small-town America or beginning an adolescent "romance," thus turning the familiar into the bizarre or the alien.

Will, the narrator of "The White Glove," is a high-school senior, describing his "romance" with a classmate, Emily Hohn. He found Emily very attractive, not despite but *because of* her ordinariness. She is day for night from his last (and first?) girlfriend, a sensuous young woman, who left him "whipped-up and feverish" (32), or sexually aroused. The last entry in his catalog of reasons for liking Emily is "she didn't stir me up—didn't move her body a certain way. I was sick to death of all that" (32–33). Clearly the boy is attempting to evade the explicitly erotic. Later, when he becomes fixated on what the white glove conceals, Emily opens her blouse and offers him her breasts, as a consolation prize for not showing him what is beneath the glove. This is the explicit eroticism Will fled from in his earlier girl friend, only to sublimate in his obsession with Emily's hand beneath the glove and in the process heighten the erotic as he has become the agent who controls it through his act of displacement.

Virtually from the beginning, Will practically *lives* with the Hohns. He finds Emily's parents appealing because they are so unlike his own parents, who are the intellectual and cultural superiors of the Hohns. The Hohn family reminds readers of 1950s families in television shows such as *Father Knows Best* or *Leave It to Beaver.* When Emily and Will are not doing homework together, they are playing Scrabble with her parents. Will particularly enjoys Mrs. Hohn, who is his peer in competitiveness.

Emily's apparent nervous tic of scratching the back of her left hand is the "snake in the garden" of this American Eden with its naturally good folks. Emily's parents have nothing explicitly sexual about them, and Will fits in so well because he is on the rebound from a romance in which his girlfriend was sexually aggressive. He is understandably relieved to go with Emily, in a relationship as overtly platonic as if Emily were a Robert.

And yet Will develops an obsession with seeing what is beneath the glove. This obsession even "justifies" his entering the Hohn house to try removing the glove from the sleeping Emily to see what it covers.[1] He fails, in part because the glove seems to resist his efforts. Indeed, it becomes for Will a monster-object with a demonic life of its own. Later, when Emily herself removes the glove for his hungry eyes, Will discovers her hand is covered with black hair. As if from contagion, he begins to feel his whole body itching and imagined that "clumps of hair were growing" (56), suggesting the story's possible investment is adolescent preoccupation with body hair as a secondary sign of sexual maturation. Eventually Will and Emily "break up," and in the end he sees her walking in town with a girlfriend.

The story's ending raises expectations of a revelation for Will. Later that afternoon at the beach, Will feels "about to understand something of immense importance, everything was about to become clear" (57), but any possible epiphany is displaced by his watching a beach ball a boy kicks into the air. Perhaps that image speaks to a new sensitivity to indeterminacy, replacing his earlier compulsion to "know" what was under the white glove.

In "Getting Closer," Millhauser takes us back to the familiar territory of a favorite subject—American boyhood. This is a rendition of boyhood, which is now "history"—likely to resonate with nostalgia for older readers but seem antique to younger readers, plugged into an electronic childhood. The title's suggestion of "getting closer," rather than getting *there,* indicates that the viewpoint character, nine-year-old Jimmy, who has looked forward all week to a family picnic, is a romantic in the Keatsian mode. On *the* day he resists beginning the experience he has anticipated because he senses that the longer he forestalls the experience by "getting closer," the more intense it will grow in his imagination. The story's ending opens out into an epiphany for Jimmy, as he finally allows himself to fall into Time, fully aware that once he accedes to time's powerful movement forward he will be locked into the downward movement toward the end of time for himself and those he loves. Short and seemingly straightforward, "Getting Closer" brilliantly demonstrates the potential magnitude of the classic *short* story in the hands of a writer like Millhauser, who is a conservator of American childhood.

The very short story "The Invasion from Outer Space" develops Millhauser's interest in science fiction. Here the "we" narrating the story appear well versed in a genre based in angst about the invasion of extraterrestrials, bent on colonizing our planet by enslaving or eradicating humanity in somewhat the way Europeans made the "New World" theirs. Rather than the expected robotic humanoids with death-rays, this "invasion" is merely a yellow dust of single-cell micro-organisms, causing a comic deflation of expectations that the invasion will bring clichéd ETs. These are just organisms intent on multiplying. What no one in the "we" chorus expects is a future in which all living creatures, including themselves, face suffocation by a yellow blob.

"People of the Book" is less a first-person narrative than a seven-page monologue to an audience of thirteen-year-olds, marking their initiation into adult knowledge. This initiation discloses the "secret" defining them as "People of the Book," a term denoting reverence for books as reflections of "*the* Book." Additionally this community literally represents the "People of the Book" as the biological descendants of books. In the Book of Legends these initiates read as children, some sections were postponed. Now they are ready to understand the *Excursus on the Copulation of Books,* in which it is written that the breath of the Creator "wrote" the Twelve Tablets, which became the First Book.

These Twelve Tablets shared the attributes of the humans later created—locomotion and copulation. Because these tablets were living beings, they lay together and produced little books, each generation reflecting the First Book, but in diminished form. Eventually a woman who fell asleep reading a tablet in the sun awoke to find she was pregnant. Clearly the "People of the Book" represent patriarchy because this "bookish" union of tablet and maiden is described as "between the spirit and the body, the word and the flesh" (71), respectively. Generations later, tablets, or books, became "sterile," or at least "impotent." This "Book" narrative begins to remind readers of the Old Testament's textuality, what with Jahweh speaking Creation into existence and later writing the Ten Commandments on the tablets Moses accepts on Mount Sinai.

In the story's second half, the speaker becomes a prophet/priest delivering a vision/sermon on Death and Life-Everlasting in the Paradise of Books. Readers, or students of the book, are bound by the Book of Laws. Initiates into adult reading already know that destroying or even mutilating a book is a capital crime. They must also learn that if they fail to resist copulating with a book their punishment will be the loss of their sexual organs. Like humans, the Book is both material and spiritual. Books may "die," that is, deteriorate or be destroyed, but they are eternal in their spiritual "life." If "The People of the Book" turn their backs on the world and dedicate themselves to studying books with a monastic reverence, they can anticipate a life hereafter as eternal students of the Book.

"The Next Thing"—longer than its three predecessors combined—returns to Millhauser's earlier interest in extravagance. As in "The Dream of the Consortium" and "Paradise Park," the author explores architectural innovations in commercial establishments, designed to induce spending. The very name—"The Next Thing"—with its self-conscious appeal to the "New" epitomizes the effort to feed the consumer's appetite for the self-gratifying confirmation of being in the vanguard of consumer culture.

In contrast to "Consortium," which drives the traditional department store upward, "The Next Thing" takes customers down into what it encourages them to nickname the "Under." There they discover aisles wide enough to drive trucks between towering "shelves" that reach toward the 180-foot ceiling. Having chosen their potential purchases electronically, customers wait for the items to land in their shopping carts, where they choose what they want to purchase. Presumably consumers have wearied of shopping online because that method seems passé—an "Old Thing."

Eventually the narrator is "consumed" by this "New Thing." Having filled out an information blank and a job application, he accepts a job offer because his fellow workers are being laid off, and "The New Thing" offers a better salary. The company buys his home and leases him an apartment in the store complex, saving him commuting time and living expenses. Eventually he discovers he has become a wage slave to a commercial enterprise, demanding more and more of his time and energy so that even after he finishes his workday he is too exhausted to do anything but rest up for the next day.

The narrator puts the best face on his entrapment by the shabby, deteriorating world of The Next Thing where maintenance is slow, if not nonexistent. Noting that a six-day work-week exhausts him, he asserts that "everyone works, you work till you drop, it's how things are" (95). Additionally he downplays the implications of The Next Thing's eradication of more traditional stores and malls, à la Walmart, and constructing more and more "Unders," rumored to be soon connected by tunnels. Despite the narrator's forced optimism—the alternative is losing his job—the future looks grim.

The novella "We Others" is a "haunting" story. At the age of fifty-two, Paul Steinbach has survived a marriage that failed in part because of the couple's inability to have children, followed by the deaths of his parents within a year, pain balanced by a successful medical practice and a renewed sense of youth and health. At bedtime he experiences chest pains and tells himself he needs "to stop working so hard" (99). When he "awoke" the next morning, he had the bizarre sensation of seeing himself in bed, not breathing.

What follows is his ghost haunting the overweight, middle-aged second-grade schoolteacher Maureen, a study in loneliness. Dismissed by her mother in favor of a younger, prettier sister, Maureen spends her evenings overeating while watching TV, especially after telephoning her mother promptly at 8:00 for a continuation of her mother's chiding her for being fat and unmarried. She had been married, but her husband left her for another teacher. Eventually Maureen becomes aware of Paul's presence in her attic, and he feels comfortable joining her in the living room, once she can not only see him but hear him speak.

These nightly conversations continue until Maureen's niece Andrea visits for a week. Andrea thinks of Maureen as her mother because Andrea's sister is also their mother's favorite, allowing Andrea to sympathize with Maureen as an unfavored sister. Maureen and Paul wait out Andrea's going to bed to continue their conversations, representing something like a "marriage" in their psychological intimacy without the intrusions of any physical connections. Unfortunately for the threesome, Paul becomes "physically" attracted to Andrea, who awakes one night to discover him in bed with her. Paul's replication of her husband's betrayal is too much for Maureen to bear, and she "evicts" him.

The story may sound like a soap opera, but it is much too complex to be easily dismissed. Its complexity lies in the reversal of expectations. Readers expect Maureen to be horrified to discover her house has become haunted, but she is lonely enough to enjoy even a ghost's company. Because sex makes relationships difficult for Maureen, Paul becomes an ideal mate. Another aspect of complexity is that Paul and "We Others" are the ones who are haunted—by the living. Indeed Paul's first encounter with an Other is compared to a fat boy encountering another fat boy he has been avoiding. Unfortunately, once again, Maureen's heart is broken when she learns that Paul cannot be content with her. Much as the elimination of sexuality ought to eradicate "sexual" jealousy, it does not for Maureen.

And finally readers—even against their will—are likely to find themselves "haunted" by "We Others." The oddity of the story's material and Millhauser's mastery as a storyteller make it difficult to resist the narrative's power in developing the loneliness and emptiness of these characters. If they are honest, readers may also be haunted by the possibility that any of us could be closer to the situations of Maureen, Andrea, and Paul, while he was alive, than they want to admit.

These "New and Selected Stories" testify to Millhauser's having clearly established himself as the major writer he has been for at least two decades, despite his absence from the best-seller lists which would make him a "household name." The "New" stories provide ample evidence of the continuing power of his imagination in bringing to readers a particularly Millhauserian take on short fiction. The "Selected" stories in the collection offer continuing expressions of his unconventional approach to doing a "retrospective," so to speak, of his work, by offering readers a smorgasbord of those stories he chose because they struck him as work he would like to read if they were written by another author.

NOTES

Chapter 1: Understanding Steven Millhauser

1. Danielle Alexander, "Steven Millhauser," *Review of Contemporary Fiction* 26.1 (Spring 2006): 7–76.

2. Review of *Dangerous Laughter,* "Upfront," *New York Times Book Review,* Oct. 5, 2008, BR6.

3. Ibid.

4. E-mail, Jan. 25, 2009.

5. Jim Shepard, "Steven Millhauser," *Bomb* (Spring 2003): 1.

6. J. D. O'Hara, "Portrait of a Romantic," *Library Journal,* Aug. 1, 1977, 1679.

7. Even though it was his first published story, "The New Automaton Theater" was held back until the later collection *The Knife Thrower* after his editor pointed out it was too similar to "August Eschenburg" for it to fit in the collection *In the Penny Arcade.*

8. E-mail, May 3, 2012. The author's remarks about the uncertainty of placing a novella should be read in the context of his success in publishing his early novellas, beginning with "August Eschenburg" in the journal *Antaeus,* which subsequently published the novella "The Princess, the Dwarf, and the Dungeon." Similarly, his novella "Catalogue of the Exhibition" appeared in *Salmagundi* and "Revenge" in *Harper's,* while "Paradise Park" was published in *Grand Street.*

9. Not coincidentally, these two stories represent half of the "Selected Stories" the author chose from his collection *Dangerous Laughter.*

10. "The Slap" is the favorite story in the collection for Michael Dirda, the *Washington Post* reviewer who has been one of the author's most appreciative readers.

11. J. D. O'Hara, "Two Mandarin Stylists," *Nation,* Sept. 17, 1977, 250–52.

Chapter 2: *Edwin Mullhouse*

1. The names "Edwin" and "Edward" are not coincidentally similar.

2. The Penn "cellar" is a forerunner of Morpheus's world.

3. It is part of the innocence of Jeffrey and Edwin's world that sexuality is totally absent, even in the boys' discourse, and no one intrudes derogatory interjections of "homo" or "faggot" to denigrate a boy for being different.

4. Jeffrey's concern with the potential deviation of seconds from the exact number past 1:06 of Edwin's birth anticipates the cataloger digressing in his narrating of the calamitous scene at the end of "Moorash" to comment on efforts to repair a damaged painting.

5. In "The Mock-Biography of Edwin Mullhouse," Adams notes Jeffrey's ominous interest in the youngest boy in the family that moved into the Mullhouse home as Jeffrey's next biographical subject.

6. E-mail message, Jan. 25, 2009.

Chapter 3: ***Portrait of a Romantic***

1. Writing in the *Library Journal,* J. D. O'Hara asserted: "This second novel proves that Millhauser's dazzling *Edwin Mullhouse* . . . was no fluke" (1679).

2. Millhauser grew up in Stratford and Fairfield, Connecticut.

3. In her extensive article in the March 2006 issue of the *Review of Contemporary Fiction,* devoted to Millhauser.

4. We find ourselves identifying the older storyteller as "Grumm" and the boy, even as an adolescent, as "Arthur" to denote his youth.

5. In the context of this "jocoserious" opening, "killer" is ambivalent: positioned after "lover," it suggests "lady-killer," but it may also be Grumm's first expression of remorse for killing his friend William Mainwaring, whose commitment to suicide he betrayed.

6. Such preservation is also the subject of Millhauser's later story "Here at the Historical Society," with its specimens of the "New Past."

7. In contrast to the fixation with dates and time in the earlier novel, time is indeterminate here. If Grumm at 29 is "writing" this novel near 1977 when it was published he might have been born about 1948 so Arthur might be meeting Philip in about 1961, a year or so before "The Sixties" began.

8. Much as Eleanor reminds readers of Poe's women, we should not forget that she is critical of Poe.

9. The author was aware that in his last years the Romantic composer Robert Schumann retreated to an insane asylum, where he died.

Chapter 4: ***From the Realm of Morpheus***

1. "Questions." E-mail of Steven Millhauser to Alicita Rodriquez, Sept. 21, 2005, cited by Alexander in "Steven Millhauser."

2. Carl Hausman's surname is one of several of Millhauser's self-conscious plays upon his own name.

3. Millhauser's interest in magicians, or "illusionists," will reach its fullest expression in "Eisenheim the Illusionist," a short story with the feel of a novella.

4. This tale is the first of numerous expressions of Millhauser's development of marital fidelity and love triangles. His later collection of novellas *The King in the Tree* offers three stories of betrayal in the eternal triangle of love.

5. Dwarves recur in Millhauser's fiction, most significantly in the novella "The Princess, the Dwarf, and the Dungeon," where the dwarf Scarbo, the only named character, moves the plot forward with his perverse machinations. Scarbo has an evil "twin" in the dwarf Modor of the novella "The King in the Tree," where he is one of three at the Court.

6. In the later novella "The Little Kingdom of J. Franklin Payne," Payne will produce a film animation of a voyage to the moon.

Chapter 5: ***In the Penny Arcade***

1. The boy who becomes "Eisenheim the Illusionist" has a similar experience which sets in motion his dedication to the art of illusion-making.

2. Mention of this first section's title reminds readers that like *Edwin Mullhouse* "August Eschenburg" has three sections. Its tripartite organization is mirrored in each of the two sections to follow with three stories, and in the tripartite organization of *In the Penny Arcade*'s Part I, novella; Part II, three stories; and Part III, three stories.

3. August is the prototype of the inventor/artist, evident also in J. Franklin Payne and Heinrich Graum.

4. Hausenstein echoes Jeffrey's cynical comment on the possible unimportance of writing Edwin's biography: "After all, there was nothing else to do" (246).

5. Much as Millhauser would impatiently deny it, readers sense in August a reflection of a serious writer's discouragement with the competition from best-seller, made-for-filming fiction, which titillates audience members and gives them an easy read.

6. Millhauser in an e-mail message, Jan. 24, 2009.

7. In his *New York Times* review, Robert Dunn notes: "Her rigid teen-age solipsism is shaken."

8. Robert Dunn sees this story as more specifically "reminiscent" of Joyce's "Araby."

9. Feminists have commented on Sigmund Freud's trope of the "dark continent" for the pudendum, and the first five letters of "cunningly" may remind the boy of the Latin *cunnus,* or vulva, in the Latinate term "cunnilingus."

10. It might be noted that the Joycean epiphany has some of this resonance of exposure. The Biblical "Epiphany" Joyce borrowed was the Feast Day celebrating the "showing forth" of the infant Jesus to the Magi. In Joyce's *Portrait of the Artist as a Young Man,* Stephen Dedalus has an epiphany of his calling as an artist after gazing at a "half-naked" girl on the beach and priding himself on responding aesthetically to her beauty rather than erotically to her sexuality.

Chapter 6: *The Barnum Museum*

1. Of "The Sisterhood of Night" Millhauser notes that "this film still isn't in production and may never be. I hope something will come of it, but so far, they've simply optioned it and are trying to raise money" (e-mail, July 18, 2012). Recently production began on the film.

2. Millhauser indicated he liked the discussion of "A Game of Clue," "which made me want to reread my own story (I almost never reread myself)" (e-mail, July 18, 2012). The latter remark is noteworthy because it underscores his extraordinary memory of details in his fiction decades after its appearance.

3. The title of Joe Orton's play, borrowed from a stereotyped pornographic film.

4. Millhauser notes: "David in this scene is a child with only a vague notion of the female body. The 'red wounds' are her nipples." The author seems to be exaggerating David's innocence at 8 (if it happened "in the year before Marian left for college, presumably at 17, nine years older than he), especially if he was interested in breasts. Surely he would have encountered pictures of statues such as the *Venus de Milo* or Renaissance paintings of nude breasts. Even if he had not, he should have generalized from his own that women's larger breasts would have larger nipples.

5. This boy's father is one of several college professors in Millhauser's fiction. Readers who know Millhauser's father was a college professor are tempted to read the experience of this movie-going boy, and other boys, as autobiographical.

6. Millhauser acknowledges not identifying the namesake of his museum, adding that "readers are right to assume it stands for P. T. Barnum." He goes on to say

it might interest you to know that there's a real Barnum Museum in Bridgeport, Connecticut, which kids in grade school in Stratford were taken to visit. I remember very little about those exhibits of the 1950s. There were costumes of General Tom Thumb and Lavinia Warren, a handkerchief which was supposed to have been in Lincoln's pocket the night he was shot, a scary skeleton, some Civil War swords. . . . Barnum is a big figure in that part of the world, since he was the mayor of East Bridgeport and built a huge house called Iranistan (which later burned to the ground). There's still a statue of Barnum in the park near Long Island Sound. (E-mail message, July 18, 2012)

7. Millhauser wrote to me: "One thing that I think no one has ever done before is connect my stories with the American 'tall tale'—a terrific insight, absolutely accurate. You'll be amused to hear that a new story by me, written last year, is called 'American Tall Tale,' and will be appearing in a month or so in *McSweeney's*" (e-mail, July 18, 2012).

8. Michiko Kakutani, "The Books of the Times," *New York Times,* June 12, 1990, 78.

9. Millhauser has done his homework, for such a political party predated the Nazi movement.

10. Jean Eugene Robert added "Houdin" with a hyphen to extend his surname, and Eric Weiss Italianized "Houdin" to become Houdini.

Chapter 7: *Little Kingdoms*

1. Of short stories and novellas, Millhauser asserts: "When I sit down to write each of them, over the course of several years, I knew in each instance that I was writing a long piece—though of course whether it would come to 50 or 60 or 100 pages couldn't be foreseen. But I knew before writing that I was dealing with something that wasn't a story of 10 or 15 or 20 pages" (e-mail, July 20, 2012).

2. Writing in *The Hudson Review,* Alan Davis sees "Payne" as "the best (and by far the longest) of the three novellas" (142). Its importance is also enhanced through its title's lending the collection the trope of "Little Kingdoms."

3. It is difficult to resist reading Horn's name as a foreshadowing of his "horning" his way into the Payne family by "horning" Payne, in the older sense of cuckolding his host, giving him horns to wear.

4. Readers are reminded that night settings figure extensively in Millhauser's work, from the climactic scene in *Edwin Mullhouse* to a ghost story such as "We Others."

5. Millhauser has indicated: "The Dornroschen fairy tale has haunted me since childhood and keeps popping up in my work" (e-mail, July 20, 2012).

6. In the spring of 2012 Millhauser asked to read my manuscript to provide corrections and suggestions, promising he would not exert control over my readings of his work. The word "melodrama" replaces my earlier term "soap opera" as the result of his pointing out that "the lives of Shelley and Byron are filled with wild melodramatic incidents only slightly less extreme than the ones I describe" (e-mail, July 20, 2012). The major difference is of course that Millhauser's Moorash is an "artist" whose accomplishments are not presented visually in this text, depriving readers of opportunities to certify the critical judgment of the cataloger-narrator, who eventually drops any pretense of genuine interest in Moorash's paintings in preference to telling this soap-opera-ish tale. Much as readers of the biographies of Shelley and Byron may

smile at the unruly lives the poets lived, they are less likely to laugh because the great poetry they left behind offers testimony to the genius of the two poets.

7. *The Sense of an Ending* is Frank Kermode's classic study of ending in narrative.

Chapter 8: *Martin Dressler*

1. Reviewers stressed Martin as the type of the tycoon. In their *New York Times Review* pieces, "Heartbreak Hotel," May 12, 1996, Janet Burroway called Martin a "bootstrap capitalist" and Laurel Graeber, June 22, 1997, spoke of him as a "Donald Trump."

2. See "The Dream of the Consortium" for the Millhauserian department store.

3. The impulse to see Martin Dressler as a plutocrat of Donald Trump's ilk recurs in R. Z. Sheppard's *Time* review, "Trump, the Early Days," June 10, 1996, in which he begins with the rhetorical question, "Why do novelists like to stereotype American entrepreneurs as single-minded and heartless?" Steven Millhauser wrote: "And you're right that the novel isn't a satire but the portrait of an overreacher, someone with whom I have immense sympathy. I remember thinking, before I began the novel: now I am going to write a book about someone as far from myself as possible, a businessman, a man of the world, an entrepreneur" (e-mail, July 27, 2012).

4. Sven Birkerts in *The Yale Review,* asserts: "Millhauser does not make his tale a tragedy" (147). But then he also believes "Millhauser begins his narrative with a generic—typifying—invocation of character . . . [so] we never get particularly close to the person" (145–46).

Chapter 9: *The Knife Thrower and Other Stories*

1. The film adaptation of "Sisterhood of Night" has gone into production.

2. See Millhauser's essay "The Fascination of the Miniature," in the summer 1983 issue of *Grand Street.*

3. Patrick McGrath, "Artists and Automatons," *New York Book Review,* May 10, 1998.

4. As in Millhauser's other fiction involving adolescents, the time setting is probably the 1950s, when the author himself was a teenager. When this story's fifteen-year-old narrator begins his night-journey, he twice mentions "ranch houses," a now somewhat old-fashioned term for one-story houses, built after WWII. Young readers may mistake "ranch houses" for a Wild West feature.

5. Millhauser wrote: "A note on 'Paradise Park.' This story—about amusement parks—was the germ of Martin Dressler. It was collected later, in *The Knife Thrower* (1998), but it was first published in a magazine in 1993 and written at least a year before that. As I was writing about Sarabee's background in the department store business, I remember thinking: this is something I need to return to, in a longer work, someday. Sarabee, as a child, even works in a cigar shop" (e-mail, July 25, 2012).

Chapter 10: *Enchanted Night*

1. Readers encounter Millhauser's own enchantment with the night in scenes from other novellas such as "Revenge" in which the widow tells the "other woman" how she stood over her at night with a kitchen knife; "An Adventure of Don Juan," in which the love-maddened Mary Hood wanders sleeplessly at night; and "The Princess, the Dwarf, and the Dungeon," in which the Princess is forced to lie in the Margrave's bed to test his honor.

2. Coop is introduced in a classically realist manner. The narrator informs readers of his age—twenty-eight—and full name—William Cooper—and prepares for his falling in love with the mannequin by suggesting it may be the result of the beer he has drunk with the "guys at Big Mama's" who call him "Coop" (29).

3. Millhauser writes: "For me, there are certainly characters in this novella, and I take them seriously, but they're rigorously subordinated to the night itself, or to Diana" (e-mail, July 27, 2012).

4. It is difficult to resist a bit of the "biographical criticism" Millhauser abhors. In the 1970s when he was not a student the author lived at home while working on *In the Realm of Morpheus,* whose manuscript ran to over a thousand pages. Also in *The Barnum Museum* story "The Invention of Robert Herendeen," the title character's father expresses frustration with supporting a son working on a big project.

Chapter 11: *The King in the Tree*

1. Zaleski's review appeared in *Publisher's Weekly* and Paddock's in *The Review of Contemporary Fiction.* Laura Miller's review, "Theme Parks of the Mind," appeared in the *New York Times Book Review,* Mar. 9, 2003, L7.

2. One feature of the species responsible for the addition of "black" to the early common name "widow spiders" is the female's habit of eating her smaller mate after mating occurs.

3. Little is known of Thomas of Britain, or Cornwall. His poem *Tristan,* telling the tale of Tristan and Iseult, survives in eight fragments, representing about one-sixth of the poem.

4. Like the court dwarf Modor, Oswin is a figure Millhauser invented for his version of the story.

5. This speculation that Thomas contributes to Tristan's death offers a parallel to other similar situations: Jeffrey's impulsively pulling the trigger to complete Edwin's "suicide," Arthur's contribution to William's proving he was a genuine "romantic," and in the present book of novellas, the widow's encouragement of her husband's possible suicide, as well as the other woman's following his escape from guilt in betraying the widow.

Chapter 12: *Dangerous Laughter*

1. Edwin Mullhouse's masterpiece was entitled *Cartoons,* and J. Franklin Payne was a cartoonist.

2. The author writes that, "like many of my 'we' narratives, the 'we' in this story deliberately shifts now and then to an 'I,' who is part of the 'we' but speaks in such instances only for himself. This double form of narration allows me to break away from the inevitable distance of 'we' to the more intimate 'I.' Thus at the end of the story, 'I too murdered Elaine Coleman' is supposed to have the force of a personal confession" (e-mail, Aug. 6, 2012).

3. The list of narratives with night settings runs literally from beginning—*Edwin Mullhouse*—to end—the title story in *We Others.*

4. In her article "Architecture and Structure in Steven Millhauser's *Martin Dressler,*" Alicita Rodríguez writes that "a close analysis of architecture reveals not only its own function within the novel, but also the greater generic impulse of the novel itself" (110).

5. "The Other Town" anticipates the concept of a "New Past" in "Here at the Historical Society."

6. The author notes: "I think early in the discussion of this story, the reader needs to be told that the tower is based on the Tower of Babel. Jehovah destroyed that tower before it reached heaven—I imagined its successful completion" (e-mail, Aug. 6, 2012).

7. There is a precedent in James Joyce's short story "A Mother" in which Joyce indicated that "Mrs. Kearney bought some lovely blush-pink charmeuse in Brown Thomas's to let into the front of Kathleen's dress" (139).

8. "Animate paint" may recall Franklin Payne's investment film animation, along with Edwin Mullhouse's *Cartoons,* Millhauser's "Cat 'n' Mouse," and his "Klassik Komix I."

Chapter 13: *We Others*

1. Readers will recall Arthur Grumm entering William Mainwaring's home at night to relieve the boredom of adolescence.

SELECTED BIBLIOGRAPHY

Works by Millhauser

NOVELS

Edwin Mullhouse: The Life and Death of an American Writer. New York: Knopf, 1972.

Portrait of a Romantic. New York: Knopf, 1977.

From the Realm of Morpheus. New York: Morrow, 1986.

Martin Dressler: The Tale of an American Dreamer. New York: Crown, 1996.

COLLECTIONS OF SHORTER FICTION

In the Penny Arcade. New York: Knopf, 1986.

The Barnum Museum. New York: Poseidon/Simon and Schuster, 1990.

Little Kingdoms. New York: Poseidon/Simon and Schuster, 1993.

The Knife Thrower and Other Stories. New York: Crown, 1998.

Enchanted Night. New York: Crown, 1999.

The King in the Tree. New York: Knopf, 2003.

Dangerous Laughter: Thirteen Stories. New York: Knopf, 2008.

We Others: New and Selected Stories. New York: Knopf, 2011.

ESSAYS

"The Fascination of the Miniature." *Grand Street* 2.4 (Summer 1983): 128–35.

"Replicas." *The Yale Review* 83 (July 1995): 50–61.

"The Ambition of the Short Story." *New York Times Book Review,* Oct. 3, 2008. http://www.nytimes.com/2008/10/05/books/review/Millhauser-t.html.

Secondary Sources

Adams, Timothy Dow. "The Mock-Biography of Edwin Mullhouse." *Biography* 5.3 (1982): 205–14.

Alexander, Danielle. "Steven Millhauser." *Review of Contemporary Fiction* 26.1 (Mar. 2006): 7–76.

Birkerts, Sven. Rev. of *Martin Dressler. Yale Review* 85.1 (1997): 144–55.

Boyd, John D. "The Double Vision of *Edwin Mullhouse.*" *Biography* 11.1 (1988): 35–46.

Burroway, Janet. "Heartbreak Hotel." *New York Times Book Review.* May 12, 1996.

Chénetier, Marc. "An Interview with Steven Millhauser." *Transatlantica: Revue D'Etudes Americaines,* 3 (2003): <http:etudes.americaines.free.fr/TRANSATLAN TICA/3/<Millhauser3.html>

Davis, Allan. "Unseen Guests." *Hudson Review* 47.1 (Spring 1994): 141–48.

Dirda, Michael. Rev. of *We Others*. *Washington Post*. Aug. 31, 2011. http://www.washingtonpost.com/entertainment/books/michael-dirda-reviews-we-others-stories-by-steven-millhauser/2011/08/24/gIQAbrwrsJ_story.html.

Dunn, Robert. "First Love and the Last Automatons." *New York Times Book Review*. Jan. 19, 1986.

Fowler, Douglas. "Steven Millhauser, Miniaturist." *Critique* 37.2 (1996): 139–48.

Graeber. Laurel. Rev. of *Martin Dressler. New York Times Book Review*. June 22, 1997.

Green, Daniel. "Two Fabulists." *Georgia Review* 49.3 (Winter 1995): 960–67.

Hebel, Udo J. "From 'Tangible Republic' to Imperial Spectacle: The Hotel World of Steven Millhauser's *Martin Dressler: The Tale of an American Dreamer*." In *Intercultural America*, ed. Alfred Hornung et al. Heidelberg, Germany: Universitatsverlag, 2007. 285–307.

Herrero-Olaizola, Alejandro. "Writing Lives; Writing Lies: The Pursuit of Apocryphal Biographies." *Mosaic* 35.3 (2002): 73–88.

Howe, Irving. "Afterword. Catalogue of the Exhibition: *The Art of Edmund Moorash (1810–1846)* by Steven Millhauser." *Salmagundi* 92 (1991): 110–14.

The Illusionist. Dir. Neil Burger. Perf. Edward Norton, Paul Giamatti. Yari Film Group. 2006.

Joyce, James. *Dubliners*. New York: Viking, 1968.

———. *A Portrait of the Artist as a Young Man*. New York: Penguin, 1993.

Kakutani, Michiko. "Books of the Times; Where Everyday Life Intersects with the Magical." *New York Times*. June 12, 1990, 78.

Kasper, Catherine. "Steven Millhauser." In *Dictionary of Literary Biography: Twenty-First Century American Novelists*. Second Series. Detroit: Gale Cengage Learning, 2009. 225–35.

Kermode, Frank. *The Sense of an Ending: Studies in the Theory of Fiction*. New York: Oxford University Press, 1967.

Kinzie, Mary. "Succeeding Borges, Escaping Kafka: On the Fiction of Steven Millhauser." *Salmagundi* 92 (1991): 115–44.

Lavoie, Thomas. Rev. of *In the Penny Arcade. Library Journal* (Jan. 1986): 103–4.

Leavitt, David. "The Unsung Voices." Rev. of *In the Penny Arcade*, by Steven Millhauser, and *Days, An Amateur Guide to the Night, and Oh!*, by Mary Robison. *Esquire* (Feb. 1986): 117–18.

McGrath, Patrick. "Artists and Automatons." *New York Times Book Review*. May 10, 1998.

Miller, Laura. "Theme Parks of the Mind." Rev. of *The King in the Tree: Three Novellas. New York Times Book Review*. Mar. 9, 2003, L7.

O'Hara, J. D. "Portrait of a Romantic." *Library Journal*. Aug. 1, 1977, 1679.

———. "Two Mandarin Stylists." *Nation*. Sep. 17, 1977, 250–52.

Paddock, Christopher. Rev. of *The King in the Tree. Review of Contemporary Fiction* 23.1 (Spring 2003): 136.

Rev. of *Dangerous Laughter. New York Times Book Review*. Oct. 5, 2008. http://www.nytimes.com/2008/10/05/books/review/Upfront-t.html.

Rodriguez, Alicita. "Architecture and Structure in Steven Millhauser's *Martin Dressler: The Tale of an American Dreamer*." *Review of Contemporary Fiction* 26.1 (2006): 110–26.

Saltzman, Arthur. "In the Millhauser Archives." *Critique* 37.2 (1996): 149–60.
Shepard, Jim. "Steven Millhauser." *Bomb* 83 (Spring 2003). http://www.nytimes.com/2008/10/05/books/review/Upfront-t.html.
Sheppard, R. Z. "Trump, the Early Days." *Time* 147.24 (June 10, 1996).
Smith, Dinitia. "Shy Author Likes to Live and Work in Obscurity." *New York Times*. Apr. 9, 1997, 13.
Zaleski, Jeff. Rev. of *The King in the Tree*. *Publisher's Weekly* 250.3 (Jan. 20, 2003).

INDEX